NORTHSTAR

Focus on Reading and Writing

Basic

Natasha Haugnes
Beth Maher

SERIES EDITORS
Frances Boyd
Carol Numrich

NorthStar: Focus on Reading and Writing, Basic

Addison Wesley Longman, 10 Bank Street, White Plains, NY 10606

Editorial director: Allen Ascher
Senior acquisitions editor: Louisa Hellegers
Development editor: Randee Falk
Director of design and production: Rhea Banker
Production manager: Marie McNamara
Managing editor: Linda Moser
Senior production editor: Christine Cervoni
Manufacturing supervisor: Edie Pullman
Photo research: Diana Nott
Cover design: Rhea Banker
Cover illustration: Robert Delaunay's *Circular Forms*, *Sun No. 2*, 1912-1913. Giraudon/Art Resource, NY. L&M Services B.V. Amsterdam 970902
Text design and composition: Delgado Design, Inc.
Text credits: **p. 84,** From "The Big Chill" by Michele Kort, *Women's Sports and Fitness*, April 1993, v.15, n.3, p. 36 "The Aquatic Ambassador: To Bring Nations Together" by Caroline Alexander, *Science World*, March 24, 1995, v.51, n.12, p. 14, and "Long Distance Swimmers: Heroic or Insane? You Make the Call" by Michael J. Scott, *Swim Magazine*, July/August 1993, v.9, n.4, p. 20; **p. 103,** "Housework" by Sheldon Harnick from *Free to Be You and Me*, McGraw Hill, 1974. Reprinted with permission from The Free To Be Foundation, Inc., LLP; **p. 184,** From *How to Improve Your Psychic Power* by Carl Rider. Copyright 1988 by Carl Rider. Published by arrangement with Carol Publishing Group. A Citadel Press Book.
Text art: Lloyd Birmingham, Ron Chironna, Dusan Petricic
Photo and art credits: **p. 1,** 1967 King Features Syndicate Inc. World rights reserved. Reprinted with special permission of King Features Syndicate; **pp. 21, 34,** maps from the US Geological Society; **p. 79,** Sports Illustrated, Time Inc.; **p. 83,** Phil Huber/Sports Illustrated, Time Inc.; **p. 119,** Christine Cervoni; **p. 139,** Tony Freeman/PhotoEdit

Library of Congress Cataloging-in-Publication Data

Maher, Elizabeth
NorthStar : Focus on reading/writing : basic / Elizabeth Maher, Natasha Haugnes.
p. cm.
ISBN 0-201-69423-9 (paperback)
1. English language—Textbooks for foreign speakers. 2. Reading comprehension—Problems, exercises, etc. 3. Report writing—Problems, exercises etc. I. Haugnes, Natasha II. Title

PE1128.M333 1998 97-43273

428.2'4—dc21 CIP

1 2 3 4 5 6 7 8 9 10—RNT—03 02 01 00 99 98

Contents

INTRODUCTION

NorthStar is an innovative four-level, integrated skills series for learners of English as a Second or Foreign Language. The series is divided into two strands: listening/speaking and reading/writing. There are four books in each strand, taking students from the Basic to the Advanced level. The two books at each level explore different aspects of the same contemporary themes, which allows for reinforcement of both vocabulary and grammatical structures. Each strand and each book can also function independently as a skills course built on high-interest thematic content.

NorthStar is designed to work alongside Addison Wesley Longman's *Focus on Grammar* series, and students are referred directly to *Focus on Grammar* for further practice and detailed grammatical explanations.

NorthStar is written for students with academic as well as personal language goals, for those who want to learn English while exploring enjoyable, intellectually challenging themes.

NORTHSTAR'S PURPOSE

The *NorthStar* series grows out of our experience as teachers and curriculum designers, current research in second-language acquisition and pedagogy, as well as our beliefs about language teaching. It is based on five principles.

Principle One: In language learning, making meaning is all-important. The more profoundly students are stimulated intellectually and emotionally by what goes on in class, the more language they will use and retain. One way that classroom teachers can engage students in making meaning is by organizing language study thematically.

We have tried to identify themes that are up-to-date, sophisticated, and varied in tone—some lighter, some more serious—on ideas and issues of wide concern. The forty themes in *NorthStar* provide stimulating topics for the readings and the listening selections, including why people like dangerous sports, the effect of food on mood, an Olympic swimmer's fight against AIDS, experimental punishments for juvenile offenders, people's relationships with their cars, philanthropy, emotional intelligence, privacy in the workplace, and the influence of arts education on brain development.

Each corresponding unit of the integrated skills books explores two distinct topics related to a single theme as the chart below illustrates.

Theme	Listening/Speaking Topic	Reading/Writing Topic
Insects	Offbeat professor fails at breeding pests, then reflects on experience	Extract adapted Kafka's "The Metamorphosis"
Personality	Shyness, a personal and cultural view	Definition of, criteria for, success

Principle Two: Second-language learners, particularly adults, need and want to learn both the form and content of the language. To accomplish this, it is useful to integrate language skills with the study of grammar, vocabulary, and American culture.

In *NorthStar*, we have integrated the skills in two strands: listening/speaking and reading/writing. Further, each thematic unit integrates the study of a grammatical point with related vocabulary and cultural information. When skills are integrated, language use inside of the classroom more closely mimics language use outside of the classroom. This motivates students. At the same time, the focus can shift back and forth from what is said to how it is said to the relationship between the two. Students are apt to use more of their senses, more of themselves. What goes on in the classroom can also appeal to a greater variety of learning styles. Gradually, the integrated-skills approach narrows the gap between the ideas and feelings students want to express in speaking and writing and their present level of English proficiency.

The link between the listening/speaking and reading/writing strands is close enough to allow students to explore the themes and review grammar and reinforce vocabulary, yet it is distinct enough to sustain their interest. Also, language levels and grammar points in *NorthStar* are keyed to Addison Wesley Longman's *Focus on Grammar* series.

Principle Three: Both teachers and students need to be active learners. Teachers must encourage students to go beyond whatever level they have reached.

With this principle in mind, we have tried to make the exercises creative, active, and varied. Several activities call for considered opinion and critical thinking. Also, the exercises offer students many opportunities for individual reflection, pair- and small-group learning, as well as out-of-class assignments for review and research. An answer key is printed on perforated pages in the back of each book so the teacher or students can remove it. A teacher's manual, which accompanies each book, features ideas and tips for tailoring the material to individual groups of students, planning the lessons, managing the class, and assessing students' progress.

Principle Four: Feedback is essential for language learners and teachers. If students are to become better able to express themselves in English, they need a response to both what they are expressing and how they are expressing it.

NorthStar's exercises offer multiple opportunities for oral and written feedback from fellow students and from the teacher. A number of open-ended opinion and inference exercises invite students to share and discuss their answers. In information gap, fieldwork, and presentation activities, students must present and solicit information and opinions from their peers as well as members of their communities. Throughout these activities, teachers may offer feedback on the form and content of students' language, sometimes on the spot and sometimes via audio/video recordings or notes.

Principle Five: The quality of relationships among the students and between the students and teacher is important, particularly in a language class where students are asked to express themselves on issues and ideas.

The information and activities in *NorthStar* promote genuine interaction, acceptance of differences, and authentic communication. By building skills and exploring ideas, the exercises help students participate in discussions and write essays of an increasingly more complex and sophisticated nature.

DESIGN OF THE UNITS

For clarity and ease of use, the listening/speaking and reading/writing strands follow the same unit outline given below. Each unit contains from 5 to 8 hours of classroom material. Teachers can customize the units by assigning some exercises for homework and/or skipping others. Exercises in sections 1–4 are essential for comprehension of the topic, while teachers may want to select among the activities in sections 5–7.

1. **Approaching the Topic**
   A warm-up, these activities introduce students to the general context for listening or reading and get them personally connected to the topic. Typically, students might react to a visual image, describe a personal experience, or give an opinion orally or in writing.

2. **Preparing to Listen/Preparing to Read**
   In this section, students are introduced to information and language to help them comprehend the specific tape or text they will study. They might read and react to a paragraph framing the topic, prioritize factors, or take a general-knowledge quiz and share information. In the vocabulary section, students work with words and expressions selected to help them with comprehension.

3. **Listening One/Reading One**
   This sequence of four exercises guides students to listen or read with understanding and enjoyment by practicing the skills of (a) prediction, (b) comprehension of main ideas, (c) comprehension of details, and (d) inference. In activities of increasing detail and complexity, students learn to grasp and interpret meaning. The sequence culminates in an inference exercise that gets students to listen and read between the lines.

4. **Listening Two/Reading Two**
   Here students work with a tape or text that builds on ideas from the first listening/reading. This second tape or text contrasts with the first in viewpoint, genre, and/or tone. Activities ask students to explicitly relate the two pieces, consider consequences, distinguish and express points of view. In these exercises, students can attain a deeper understanding of the topic.

5. **Reviewing Language**
   These exercises help students explore, review, and play with language from both of the selections. Using the thematic context, students focus on language: pronunciation, word forms, prefixes and suffixes, word domains, idiomatic expressions, analogies. The listening/speaking strand stresses oral exercises, while the reading/writing strand focuses on written responses.

6. **Skills for Expression**
   Here students practice related grammar points across the theme in both topics. The grammar is practiced orally in the listening/speaking strand, and in writing in the reading/writing strand. For additional practice, teachers can turn to Addison Wesley Longman's *Focus on Grammar*, to which *NorthStar* is keyed by level and grammar points. In the Style section, students practice functions (listening/speaking) or rhetorical styles (reading/writing) that prepare them to express ideas on a higher level. Within each unit, students are led from controlled to freer practice of productive skills.

7. **On Your Own**
   These activities ask students to apply the content, language, grammar, and style they have practiced in the unit. The exercises elicit a higher level of speaking or writing than students were capable of at the start of the unit. Speaking topics include role plays, surveys, presentations, and experiments. Writing topics include paragraphs, letters, summaries, and academic essays.

In Fieldwork, the second part of On Your Own, students go outside of the classroom, using their knowledge and skills to gather data from personal interviews, library research, and telephone or Internet research. They report and reflect on the data in oral or written presentations to the class.

AN INVITATION

We think of a good textbook as a musical score or a movie script: It tells you the moves and roughly how quickly and in what sequence to make them. But until you and your students bring it to life, a book is silent and static, a mere possibility. We hope that *NorthStar* orients, guides, and interests you as teachers.

It is our hope that the *NorthStar* series stimulates your students' thinking, which in turn stimulates their language learning, and that they will have many opportunities to reflect on the viewpoints of journalists, commentators, researchers, other students, and people in the community. Further, we hope that *NorthStar* guides them to develop their own viewpoint on the many and varied themes encompassed by this series.

We welcome your comments and questions. Please send them to us at the publisher:

Frances Boyd and Carol Numrich, Editors
NorthStar
Addison Wesley Longman
10 Bank Street
White Plains, NY 10606-1951
or, by e-mail at:
aw/elt@awl.com

ACKNOWLEDGMENTS

We extend a huge thanks to Carol Numrich for everything—her guidance, enthusiasm, feedback, tact, patience, humor, commitment, and vision.

We would also like to thank Allen Ascher, Randee Falk, and Christine Cervoni at Addison Wesley Longman for their help in seeing this project through.

We're grateful to Matt Burry and Donna Dager for Web researching help, and to Kate Griffeath at the Academy of Art College for her all around support and enthusiasm.

Beth appreciates the time Tom Darci, her husband, put into running the household while she was at the computer. Also, we both thank him for being our administrative assistant, proofreader, sounding board, and moral support.

Natasha thanks Dr. Pat Porter at San Francisco State University for preparing and inspiring her to undertake this project.

Natasha Haugnes and Beth Maher

UNIT 1

FINDING THE IDEAL JOB

1 APPROACHING THE TOPIC

A. PREDICTING

Look at the cartoon and read the information. Discuss your answers to the questions.

In the United States today, many people make midlife[1] career changes.[2] After many years at one kind of work, they change to a different kind of work.

1. **Why does the man in the cartoon want to make a midlife career change?**
2. **Do you know people who have changed careers? Why did they change careers?**
3. **Is it easy or hard to change careers? Explain your answer.**

[1]*midlife:* the time in the middle of a person's life, in or near the forties

[2]*career change:* a change from one kind of work to another, for example, from teaching to selling

B. SHARING INFORMATION

Read the statements. How much do you agree or disagree? For each statement, circle a number. Discuss your answers with your classmates.

	STRONGLY AGREE	AGREE	DISAGREE	STRONGLY DISAGREE	
a.	1	2	3	4	Enjoying your work is more important than making a lot of money.
b.	1	2	3	4	Working with a lot of people is better than working alone.
c.	1	2	3	4	Working from home is better than working at an office.
d.	1	2	3	4	Working indoors is better than working outside.

2 PREPARING TO READ

A. BACKGROUND

Read the charts on page 3. In a small group, discuss the questions that follow.

Are people happy with their jobs? Studies on ***job satisfaction*** (happiness in your job) suggest some interesting answers to this question.

According to Study 1, 65 percent of American workers are satisfied with their jobs. Study 2 suggests that even fewer Americans are satisfied.

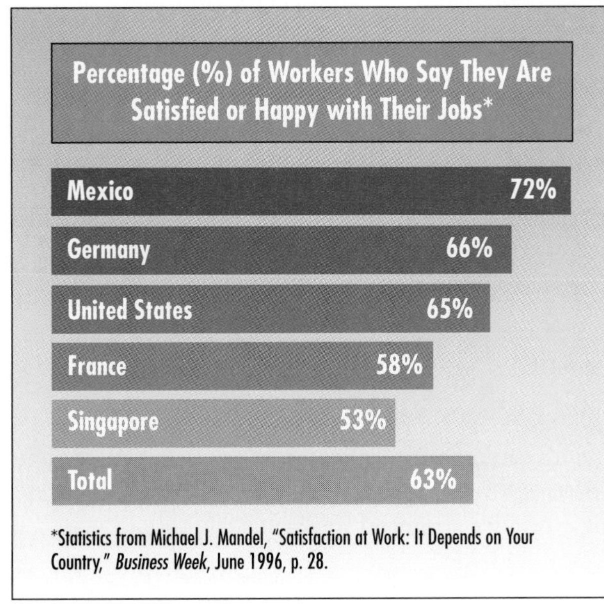

Study 1

Percentage (%) of Americans Who Think They Chose the Wrong Career*

Men 38%
Women 50%
Total 42%

*Elizabeth Fenner, "Take the Pizza, Shove the Job," *Money Magazine*, March 1994, p. 82.

Study 2

1. According to the first study, of these five countries, the country with the most job satisfaction is ________. According to the study, of these five countries, the one with the least job satisfaction is ________.

2. According to the first study, for these five countries together, 63 percent of workers are satisfied with their jobs. Does this number surprise you? Why or why not?

3. The second study is about Americans who think they chose the wrong career. Someone who is not satisfied might want to change jobs but not change careers. What is the difference between changing your job and changing your career?

4. In the second study, why do you think there are differences between men and women in job satisfaction?

5. What would you do if you felt unsatisfied with your career?

B. VOCABULARY FOR COMPREHENSION

Read the words and phrases and their definitions listed below. Then complete the sentences using these words or phrases. The first one has been done for you.

advice: suggestions about what to do

career: the kind of work a person does, usually after learning how and usually for a long time

expert: a person who knows a lot about something

hire: to give someone a job

interview: a conversation where a person looking for a job is asked a lot of questions by a person looking for a new worker

manager: the person in charge of a group of workers

out of work: having no job

résumé: a piece of paper with your work and education history

rewards: good things you get in return for work (such as money or health insurance)

skill: something that you can do well; ability

update: to change by putting in new information

want ads: advertisements, usually in a newspaper, for jobs that are available

1. In 1930, jobs were hard to find. Almost 25 percent of all Americans were __out of work__.
2. He has fifteen years of experience working with electric cars. Many people think he's a(n) __expert__.
3. He's had many different jobs, but only one __career__. In other words, he's worked in many different schools, but he's always been a teacher.
4. Most companies ask for a(n) __resume__ so they can read about you before they talk to you in person.
5. She sells a lot of her paintings. She has a lot of __skills__ as an artist and a businesswoman.
6. She was offered two jobs at the same time. She didn't know what to do. So she asked me for __advice__.
7. Let's __hire__ Katlyn. She has the most experience. She will be a great teacher.

8. She needed a job, so she decided to look at the want ads.
9. The rewards of her job just weren't enough. She was happy with the work, but she wasn't making enough money.
10. When looking for a job, it's important to update your résumé. Write down your most recent jobs and education.
11. She was a computer programmer for ten years. Then she became a(n) manager. Suddenly, she had to lead all the people she used to work with.
12. Kristin had a(n) interview for a job yesterday. She was very nervous, but I think she got the job.

3 READING ONE: Finding the Ideal Job

A. INTRODUCING THE TOPIC

Imagine you are not satisfied with your job. You decide to ***job hunt****—that is, to look for a new job. With a partner write a list of things you might do to find a job. The first one has been done for you.*

1. I might ask someone in my family for a job.
2. ______
3. ______
4. ______
5. ______
6. ______
7. ______
8. ______

Now learn what a professional has to say about this topic. Read "Finding the Ideal Job," a book review of What Color Is Your Parachute? *(A book review is an article in a magazine or newspaper that tells people about a new book. Usually a review explains the main ideas of a book and gives an opinion about the book.)*

Finding the Ideal Job. Review of *What Color Is Your Parachute?*

by Barbara Kleppinger

1 You are out of work.

You hate your job.

You aren't satisfied with your career.

You are looking for your first job. Where do you start?

2 If you are like most Americans, you'll probably send your résumé to a lot of companies. You might answer newspaper want ads every Sunday. Or you might go to employment agencies. But experts say you won't have much luck. People find jobs only five to fifteen percent of the time when they use these methods. So, what can you do?

3 One thing you can do is read Richard Nelson Bolles's *What Color Is Your Parachute*[1]*? A Practical Manual for Job Hunters and Career Changers*. Bolles is an expert in the field of job hunting. He has helped thousands of people find jobs and careers. This book is different from other job-hunting manuals. Bolles doesn't help you to find just another job. Instead, he helps you find your ideal job: a job that fits who you are, a job that is satisfying to *you*. What kind of job is ideal for you? If you don't know the answer, Bolles says, you can't find your ideal job. You need to have a clear picture in your mind of the job you want. The book has many exercises to help you draw this picture.

4 Bolles says that you must think about three things:

(1) *Your skills*. What do you like to do? What do you do well? Do you like talking? Helping people? Teaching? Reading and writing? Using computers? Working with your hands? Bolles asks you to think about all your skills, not only "work skills." For example, a mother of four children is probably good at managing people (children!). She may be a good manager.

(2) *Job setting*. Where do you like to work? Do you like to work outside? At home? In an office? Alone or with others? What kind of people do you like to work with?

(3) *Job rewards*. How much money do you need? How much money do you want? What else do you want from a job? What would make you feel good about a job?

5 After Bolles helps you decide on your ideal job, he gives you specific, useful advice on how to find the job. His exercises teach you how to find companies and how to introduce yourself. The chapter on job interviews is full of useful information and suggestions. For example, most people go to interviews asking themselves the question "How do I get the company to hire me?" Bolles thinks this is the wrong question. Instead, he wants you to ask yourself, "Do I really want to work for this company?"

6 There are two small problems with the book. First, Bolles writes too much! He explains some of his ideas over and over again. Second, there is no space to write the answers to the exercises. But these are small problems. *What Color Is Your Parachute?* is the best job-hunting manual available today.

7 *What Color Is Your Parachute?* was written in 1970. But the information is updated every year. So, if you are looking for a job, or if you have a job but want a new one, remember: Don't just send out copies of your résumé. Don't just answer want ads. And don't wait for friends to get you a job. Instead, buy this book and do a job hunt the right way.

---

[1]*parachute*: something you wear when you jump out of a plane. When you jump, it opens up and it stops you from hitting the ground very hard.

B. READING FOR MAIN IDEAS

Decide if the sentences are true or false. Write T or F next to each sentence. Compare your answers with a classmate's.

____ **1.** *What Color Is Your Parachute?* is similar to other job-hunting manuals.

____ **2.** Bolles's goal is to help people find jobs as quickly as possible.

____ **3.** According to *What Color Is Your Parachute?*, job hunters should think about their skills, the work setting, and the job rewards they want.

____ **4.** *What Color Is Your Parachute?* includes specific advice on finding jobs.

____ **5.** According to the reviewer, one problem of the book is that it's too short.

C. READING FOR DETAILS

Write the job-hunting methods listed below in the correct column in the chart. The first one has been done for you.

answer newspaper want ads
ask friends to help find a job
decide what kind of job is ideal
think about job rewards
do exercises
go to an employment agency
decide what kind of place you want to work in
~~send out lots of résumés~~
think about your skills

WHAT MANY PEOPLE DO TO FIND A JOB	WHAT BOLLES SAYS WILL HELP YOU FIND A JOB
send out lots of résumés	

D. READING BETWEEN THE LINES

Read each situation. Decide whether, according to Bolles, the person is making a mistake or doing the right thing. Circle your answer. Then discuss your decisions with your classmates.

1. Owen was always a manager. He doesn't want to be a manager. But he's not looking for another job because he thinks that he doesn't know how to do anything else. According to Bolles, Owen is
a. making a mistake.
b. doing the right thing.

2. Amy studied to be a teacher. But now she's not just looking for work as a teacher. Instead, she's thinking about whether teaching is really the right career for her. According to Bolles, Amy is
a. making a mistake.
b. doing the right thing.

3. Bill is in a job interview. He is asking the person who is interviewing him some questions about the company. According to Bolles, Bill is
a. making a mistake.
b. doing the right thing.

4. Kathy has a choice between a job that pays very well and a job that seems very interesting. She decides that for her, money is the most important thing. So she chooses the job that pays well. According to Bolles, Kathy is
a. making a mistake.
b. doing the right thing.

5. Peter sent his résumé to many companies and he answered many want ads. So now he is waiting for someone to call him about a job. According to Bolles, Peter is
a. making a mistake.
b. doing the right thing.

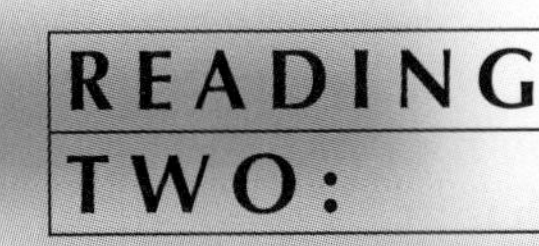

READING TWO: The Ideal Job

A. EXPANDING THE TOPIC

Read the stories and complete the sentences on page 10.

The Ideal Job

1 Believe it or not, some people get paid—and well—for doing the things that make them really happy. Here are a few people who have found the job of their dreams.

"I know all about job-hunting."—Betsy

2 A few years ago, I lost my job as a manager in a factory. I was so unhappy. I was thirty-eight years old, out of work for the 100th time, and without much hope. Then, one day I was thinking about the question, "What do I do best?" and the answer came to me. I had been out of work many times, so I knew every manual about how to find a job or change a career. I must have been to over 100 interviews in my life, made 1,000 phone calls asking for jobs, and sent out a résumé to almost 2,000 companies. When I looked at my skills, I saw that my best skills were job-hunting skills! So I started my own company, Career Consulting. It's a business that helps people find jobs. I hired two people to work with me. The three of us work together on everything, but I'm the boss. It's great. I love the work, and I make a lot of money!

"I have the funnest job in the world."—Amanda

3 I have been a matchmaker for forty-one years. Because of me, sixty couples are now happily married or engaged. I'm a good matchmaker. I have a very good eye for people. And I don't mean I match people on how they look. I mean I can meet a person just once for ten minutes, and I know for sure what kind of person he or she is. I get a feeling. And this feeling tells me, "Oh, he would be a great husband for Stephanie," or "Ah, now here is the woman for Timothy." I can't imagine a job that's more fun. I meet wonderful people. I work for

myself. Nobody tells me what to do. I make enough money to live a simple life. And I get so much joy from seeing what happens to my matches. A month ago a couple stopped by on their way home from the hospital with their new baby girl. I'm so happy to think that I helped make that family!

"I have a job with an incredible view."—Donna

4 Teaching skydiving is so exciting. I love seeing students on their first jump. They are all nervous and excited. When they get to the ground, they can't wait to call everyone they know and tell them they just jumped out of an airplane. Later, when they learn to turn and fly forward, they realize that they're not just a flying stone. They realize that they're like a bird—they can fly!

5 It wasn't easy to get this job. I had to have about 1,000 jumps and about two years of training. And the salary was only $15,000 for the first year. But I don't do it for the money. In fact, I don't need to get paid at all. I love it that much!

Adapted from "From Sky Diving Instructors to Fashion Consultants, Some Folks Just Love Their Jobs" by Dave Curtin, Knight-Ridder/Tribune News Service, 11 March 1996, p. 311K619.

Complete the sentences with the correct name from the reading. The first one has been done for you.

1. ___Donna___ made $15,000 a year.
2. ____________ helped sixty couples find each other.
3. ____________ was out of work many times.
4. ____________ has had the same job for over forty years.
5. ____________ changed careers.
6. ____________ loves teaching.

B. LINKING READINGS ONE AND TWO

Look back at the review of What Color Is Your Parachute? *Reread the paragraphs about skills, setting, and rewards and the questions in each paragraph. How would the women in the reading answer the questions? Write answers for each woman. The first one has been done for you.*

1. Betsy

Skills: I have a lot of job-hunting skills.

Setting: ____________________

Rewards: ____________________

2. Amanda

Skills: ____________________

Setting: ____________________

Rewards: ____________________

3. Donna

Skills: ____________________

Setting: ____________________

Rewards: ____________________

4. What about you? How do you answer these questions?

Your name: ____________________

Skills: ____________________

Setting: ____________________

Rewards: ____________________

5 REVIEWING LANGUAGE

A. EXPLORING LANGUAGE

Cross out the word or phrase that is not related to the boldfaced word. The first one has been done for you.

1. **résumé:** work history, job hunting, ~~money~~
2. **want ad:** newspaper, skill, job
3. **employment agency:** secretary, job hunt, résumé
4. **career:** city, work, experience

5. **sky diver:** plane, water, jump
6. **out of work:** job hunting, manager, free time
7. **engaged:** plan, school, ring
8. **manual:** book, information, newspaper
9. **interview:** company, answers, computers
10. **advice:** information, suggestions, exercises
11. **boss:** owner, manager, job hunter

B. WORKING WITH WORDS

Complete the e-mail from Cristina to Jenny with the words below.

hire interview out of work résumé skills specific

From: Cristina_Bond@Richmond.edu
Sent: 01 July 1998 14:23
To: JRIOS@aol.com
Subject: New Job :)

Hi Jenny,

Guess what? I finally found a job. I'm so excited! I thought I was going to be **(1)**_______________ forever. I was so nervous during the **(2)**_______________. I was sure they didn't want to **(3)**___________________ me. At first they asked me lots of general questions about my life. That information was on my **(4)**___________________. But then they started to ask me lots of **(5)**______________ questions about computers. I'm so glad I took that Internet course last summer. It gave me a lot of computer **(6)**______________ that I can use at this job. Wow, I can't believe it. I'll call you next week with my new work number.

Yours,
Web Master[1] Cristina

[1] *Web Master:* the job title for people who design Internet web pages

6

SKILLS FOR EXPRESSION

A. GRAMMAR: Descriptive Adjectives and Possessive Adjectives

1 *Read the e-mail from Cristina to Jenny. Notice the underlined words. They are two kinds of adjectives: descriptive adjectives and possessive adjectives.*

From: Cristina_Bond@Richmond.edu
Sent: 13 October 1998 9:12
To: JRIOS@aol.com
Subject: Old Job :(

Hey Jenny,

A <u>bad</u> thing happened to me last week. NetMakers was sold, and I lost <u>my</u> <u>new</u> job. NetMakers is a <u>small</u> company, so I knew this might happen. But I didn't think it would happen so fast! It was such a <u>great</u> job for me because I could use <u>my</u> skills. And the job was <u>fun</u>. I guess I'll have to start job hunting again. How about <u>your</u> job? How is it going? The last time we talked, you were <u>bored</u>. Is <u>your</u> job <u>interesting</u> now? Don't e-mail me at this address anymore. Just call me on <u>my</u> home phone.

Cristina

List each adjective in the e-mail on one of the lines. The first ones have been done for you.

1. Descriptive adjectives: bad, ______
2. Possessive adjectives: my, ______

FOCUS ON GRAMMAR

See Descriptive Adjectives and Possessive Adjectives in *Focus on Grammar, Basic.*

Descriptive and Possessive Adjectives

Descriptive adjectives describe nouns. They can come after the verb *be.*	She is **smart.**
They can come before a noun.	She is a **smart** teacher.
When a noun follows an adjective, use *a, an,* or *the* before the adjective. (*A* and *an* are used only with count nouns; see Unit 7.)	She's **a smart** teacher. She's **an important** writer. **The new** teacher isn't here.
Remember: Do **not** use *a, an,* or *the* when the adjective is not followed by a noun.	Gary is smart.
Possessive adjectives show belonging.	I have a job. **My** job is very interesting.
A noun always follows a possessive adjective. When using possessive adjectives, do not use *a, an,* or *the.*	**His** boss is nice.
Possessive adjectives have the same form before singular or plural nouns.	**Your** paintings are beautiful. **Your** painting is beautiful.

Possessive Adjectives

my your his her its our your their

2 *Use the words to write sentences. The first one has been done for you.*

1. for/Jenny/a/is/career/looking/new Jenny is looking for a new career.
2. like/She/job/didn't/old/her ______
3. Our/manager/was/old/nice ______
4. want ads/job/his/Juan/new/found/in/the ______
5. sister/out/work/of/is/My ______
6. an/Nelson Bolles/job/interesting/has ______

3 *Look at the pictures that follow. Write about the work that the people do, how the people are feeling, and how they look. For each picture, write at least three sentences. For each picture, use at least one possessive adjective, one descriptive adjective before a noun, and one descriptive adjective after* **be**. *You can use the descriptive adjectives listed below. The first one has been done for you.*

big	dirty	hungry	messy	sad	sleepy	young
curly	happy	long	old	short	straight	

1. The man:

He is a young man. He has short hair. He is hungry. He drives an old truck.

The truck:

His truck is old. The old truck is dirty.

2. The woman:

____

____

The desk:

____

____

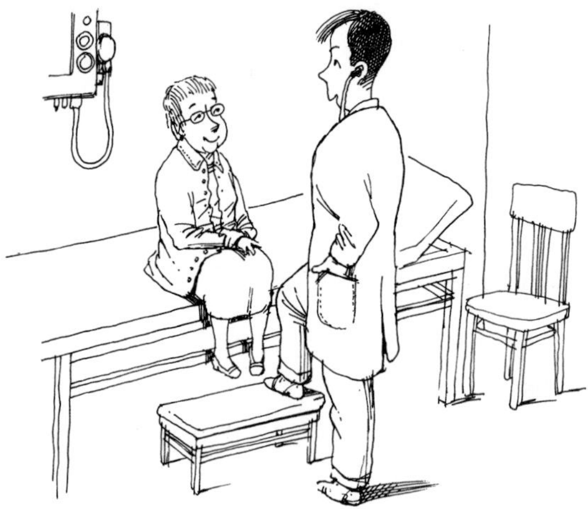

3. The doctor:

____

____

The patient:

____

____

B. STYLE: The Sentence

❶ *Read the following lines and then answer the questions.*

1. Marika worked for a big camera company for six years.

2. My friend in Boston.

3. Eli works twenty hours a week.

4. He's tired.

5. Teaches mathematics to college students in Massachusetts.

Which ones are sentences? Which aren't sentences? How do you know?

Parts of the Sentence

◆ Every sentence in English must have a subject and a verb. A sentence can have just a subject and a verb. But, usually, sentences have other words, too.	He (subject) cooks (verb).
◆ In commands we don't say or write a subject. But the subject of commands is always understood as "you."	Stop that! = You stop that.
◆ Subjects come before the verb and often come at the beginning of the sentence.	**Everybody** (subject) told me it was a great job.
◆ Subjects can be one word or many words.	**Everybody** (subject) told me it was a great job. **My uncle, my sister, and all my friends** (subject) told me it was a great job.
◆ Subjects can't be repeated.	WRONG: **Connie** (S1) she (S2) told me it was a great job.
◆ The first letter of the first word of a sentence must be capitalized.	**T**here was one problem.
◆ A sentence must end with a period, question mark, or exclamation point.	I was bored**.**
◆ Some verbs (like *laugh*) don't have objects. Some verbs (like *hire*) have one object. Some verbs (like *give*) have two objects.	She laughed (verb). The company hired (verb) **Tadashi** (object). The company gave (verb) **him** (object) **the job** (object).

2 *Each sentence has one mistake. Correct the mistakes. The first one has been done for you.*

1. The camera company ~~it~~ paid Marika a lot of money.
2. She happy with her job at the camera company.
3. Decided to change her job anyway.
4. Her friends told to stay with the camera company.
5. they didn't understand her decision.
6. Why did she change her job
7. Marika she just wanted her dream job.
8. Started Marika her own restaurant.
9. Marika happier now than ever before!

3 *Write five sentences to describe someone's job—for example, your job, your father's job, or a friend's job.*

Example: My friend Jennifer is a kindergarten teacher. Her job is very hard. She is tired every day. But her job is also a lot of fun. Her job does not pay a lot of money.

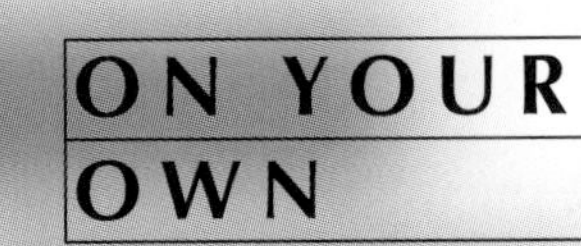

7 ON YOUR OWN

A. WRITING TOPICS

Choose one of the following topics. Write one or two paragraphs. Use some of the vocabulary, grammar, and style that you learned in this unit. Be sure to write correct sentences.

1. Imagine your friend just finished college and doesn't know what to do for work. Write him or her a short note with advice. Use information from the review of *What Color Is Your Parachute?* You can also use your list on page 5. Give your friend at least three suggestions.

2. Do you know anyone who has found his or her dream job? Write about this person. Answer these questions: Who is he or she? What does he or she do? How did he or she get the job? What is most important to him or her about the job?

3. Imagine you have your dream job. What do you do? Describe your job. Be sure to discuss the three things that Nelson Bolles says are important: the skills you use, the setting, and the rewards.

B. FIELDWORK

In pairs, interview someone who may want to change careers. This person might be your classmate, your teacher, your neighbor, or a relative.

1. Ask this person questions about his or her career dreams. You should start with the following questions. If you want, add some questions of your own to the list.

   a. What is your name?
   b. What is your career now?
   c. What do you do in your career?
   d. What are the good and bad things about your career?
   e. What kind of career do you want to have? Why?
   f. Why would you like this dream career better than your career?

   g. ______________________________

   h. ______________________________

2. Interview the person.

3. After the interview, write a report. Describe the job that person has and the job that he or she wants. Explain why he or she dreams about a different kind of career. Use any ideas you learned from the readings to help you write.

4. Share your report with your classmates. Discuss the stories and information in the reports. What do people want from a career?

UNIT 2

GUARDING NATURE WITH GREENBELTS

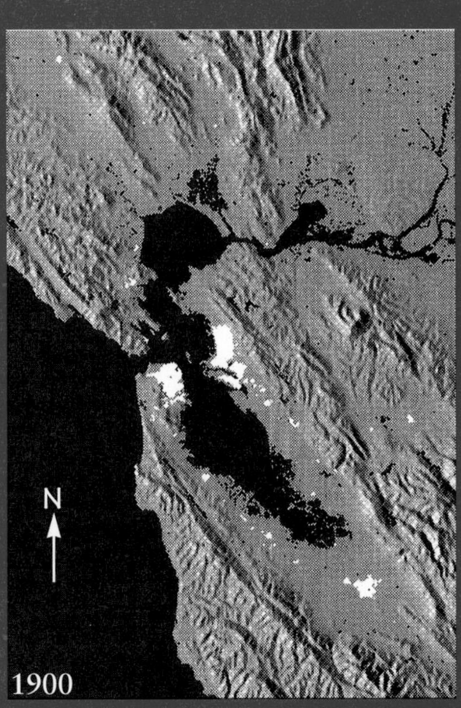

1 APPROACHING THE TOPIC

A. PREDICTING

Look at the two maps of the San Francisco Bay Area. The white areas show where the cites and towns are. The black area is water, San Francisco Bay. Discuss your answers to the questions.

1. **San Francisco (on the west side of the bay), Oakland (on the east side) and San Jose (on the south side) were the three biggest cities on the map in 1900. Can you find them?**
2. **Can you find these three cities on the map from 1990?**
3. **What do you think was between these three cities in 1900?**
4. **What was between them in 1990?**
5. **What do you think a map from 2050 will look like?**

B. SHARING INFORMATION

Write your answers to the following questions about nature areas. Nature areas can be parks, beaches, forests, or any other area where there is more nature than buildings. The first four questions are about where you are living now. The next four questions are about where you lived when you were a child. Compare answers with a partner.

Now . . .

1. What are the nature areas nearest to your home? ___________________

____

2. Do you go there? ____
3. What do you do there? ____

____

4. Do you think these are important places? Why or why not? _________

____

In the past . . .

5. What were the nature areas nearest to your home when you were young?

____

____

____

6. Did you go there? ____
7. What did you do there? ____

____

8. Are these places still nature areas, or have they changed? ___________

____

2

PREPARING TO READ

A. BACKGROUND

Read the information. Then in small groups, answer the questions that follow.

In the United States, before the 1940s, most people lived in cities and towns, or on farms. If they weren't farmers, they built their houses close to town centers because they wanted to be near shops, schools, and jobs. But, in the 1940s, more people started to buy cars. With cars, people traveled everywhere easily, so they didn't need to live close to city or town centers anymore. People who worked in cities moved out of the cities to nearby areas. Suburbs began to grow.

In the years that followed, more and more suburbs grew around cities. They grew so much that they touched each other and there were no more large nature areas between them. They are still growing. We use the phrase "suburban sprawl" to describe an area where many suburbs or towns touch each other.

1. Where did people like to live in the early 1900s? Why?

2. Where did many people begin to move in the 1940s? Why were they able to move there?

3. What used to be between cities?

4. What is often between cities now?

5. Do you have suburban sprawl where you live now?

6. Can you think of places that have suburban sprawl?

B. VOCABULARY FOR COMPREHENSION

Read the sentences. Use the underlined words to complete the definitions that follow. The first one has been done for you.

- Hal has an acre of land behind his house. There is enough space for about four more houses.
- One benefit to living in the country is that it is usually quieter than a city.
- If they cut down the forest to build new houses, many of the birds will disappear.
- Town centers usually include banks, shops, schools, post offices, and restaurants.
- My dad loves to take his dogs for walks on the open land near his house.
- Many people live in the suburbs but work in cities.
- In the area around Los Angeles, it is difficult to know where one town ends and another town begins because there is a lot of suburban sprawl.
- I love urban areas. I've lived in London, Tokyo, and Chicago.

1. ____Urban____ areas are cities.
2. ____________ are areas with houses, just outside cities.
3. If things ____________, they are not there anymore.
4. ____________ happens when suburbs and towns grow into each other.
5. To ____________ means to have as a part of.
6. An ____________ is a measure of land; it equals 43,560 square feet.
7. A ____________ is a good thing or good result.
8. ____________ has few or no buildings on it.

3

READING ONE: About the Bay Area's Greenbelt and Greenbelt Alliance

A. INTRODUCING THE TOPIC

The following brochure is from Greenbelt Alliance, an organization in the San Francisco Bay Area. This group of people is working to save a "greenbelt." What do you think a greenbelt is? Discuss this question with a partner. Then read the brochure to see if your answers are correct.

About the Bay Area's Greenbelt and Greenbelt Alliance

1 **What is the Bay Area's Greenbelt?**
The Greenbelt is a wide belt of open land around the cities and towns of the San Francisco Bay Area. The Bay Area Greenbelt is one of the largest areas of open land in any U.S. urban area.

2 **How big is the Greenbelt?**
The Greenbelt includes about 3.75 million of the Bay Area's 4.5 million acres. The other 731,000 acres are urban or suburban. San Francisco, for example, covers 30,000 acres; Santa Rosa covers 22,000 acres; San Jose covers more than 100,000 acres.

3 **What is the "open land" in the Greenbelt?**
Open land is land that has few buildings and lots of natural areas. The Greenbelt's open land includes parks, forests, beaches, and more than 8,500 farms.

4 **What are the benefits of the Greenbelt?**
The Greenbelt has many benefits for people in the Bay Area, which include:

- walking, camping, and biking areas close to the cities and towns
- places for wild plants and animals
- cleaner air and water
- separate towns (it stops towns from growing together)
- income from farms.

5 **Is the Greenbelt in danger?**
Five hundred seventy thousand acres of the Greenbelt are in danger. There are builders who want to build suburbs on them. If those acres become suburbs, many things will change:

- the urban and suburban area will almost double
- many farms will disappear
- traffic will become worse
- the air will become dirtier
- many beautiful forested hills will have houses on them.

6 **What is Greenbelt Alliance?**
Greenbelt Alliance is an organization that saves land in the San Francisco Bay Area. It began in 1958. We help to save the area's Greenbelt of open space. We also help to make our cities and towns better places to live.

7 **How does Greenbelt Alliance help save the Greenbelt?**
Greenbelt Alliance works alone and with other groups to save the Greenbelt in four ways:

1. We try to convince people to build new buildings on land that is already urban, not on open land.
2. We make sure that the city and town governments are all making plans to save the Greenbelt.
3. We help Bay Area towns and cities to buy pieces of open land to make into nature areas.
4. We teach people in the Bay Area why the Greenbelt is important and what they can do to help save it.

8 **How can I get involved with Greenbelt Alliance?**
You can become a member for $35. Or you can go on one of our Greenbelt Trips (free walks, bike rides, and farm tours). You can also become a volunteer. For more information, call us at
1-800-543-GREEN.

B. READING FOR MAIN IDEAS

Choose the best ending for each sentence.

1. A greenbelt is . . .
   a. open land around an urban area.
   b. a group of parks in a city.
   c. a group of people who try to save nature areas.
2. The Greenbelt Alliance is an organization that . . .
   a. helps people build better cities closer together.
   b. saves land around an urban and suburban area.
   c. takes people on walks, bike rides, and other trips.
3. The Greenbelt Alliance tries to work. . .
   a. with builders, governments, and people who live in the San Francisco Bay Area.
   b. against builders, but with governments.
   c. with schools and volunteers.

C. READING FOR DETAILS

The following statements are false. Change one word or phrase in each statement to make it true. There is more than one possible answer for some statements. The first one has been done for you.

1. The Bay Area's Greenbelt is a belt of open land ~~in~~ around the cities and towns of the San Francisco Bay Area.
2. The size of the San Francisco Bay Area is 3.75 million acres.
3. The largest city in the San Francisco Bay Area is San Francisco.
4. The whole Greenbelt is in danger.

5. The open land will almost double if 570,000 acres of the Greenbelt become suburbs.

6. The Greenbelt Alliance tries to convince people to build on open land.

7. If you want to become a Greenbelt Alliance volunteer, you must pay $35.

D. READING BETWEEN THE LINES

Circle the number next to each project that you think the Greenbelt Alliance might agree with. Discuss your answers in small groups.

1. A builder wants to build two new apartment buildings on open land in San Francisco.

2. The government of Alameda (next to San Francisco) wants to sell some land on a large open hill to a builder because Alameda needs money for schools.

3. Some people want to build a new highway from the suburbs into San Francisco so that they can drive to work faster.

4. San Francisco wants to build a new fast train from the west side of the city to the downtown area.

5. A group of volunteers wants to invite several hundred people to a three-day meeting in San Francisco to learn about California's plants and animals.

6. The National Park Service wants to build a campground in the redwood forest north of San Francisco.

READING TWO: Kenya's Greenbelt Movement

A. EXPANDING THE TOPIC

Greenbelts exist all over the world. You learned about the San Francisco Bay Area's Greenbelt. Now read about a greenbelt in Africa. Write your answers to the questions that follow. Share your answers with a partner.

Kenya's Greenbelt Movement

1 Kenya's greenbelt movement started in 1977, when a woman named Wangari Maathai decided to help save the forests in Kenya. In Kenya, many people cut down trees because they need wood to burn for cooking and heating. But when all the trees are cut down, the forest doesn't grow back. Then people have no more wood. Eventually, if no trees are replanted, the area becomes desert. Wangari started growing and selling young trees in her garden for people to plant in places where they cut down trees. Soon, other women became involved and began to grow trees to sell, too.

2 Today in Kenya there are more than 1,500 people selling young trees, and more than 10 million trees have been planted. Twelve other African countries have started greenbelt projects like Kenya's.

1. Why did Wangari Maathai start the greenbelt movement? ____________

____

2. What happens to the land if all of the trees are cut down and nobody plants more trees? ______________________________

____

B. LINKING READINGS ONE AND TWO

Complete the chart. Then in small groups, discuss your answers to the questions that follow.

	SAN FRANCISCO'S GREENBELT ALLIANCE	KENYA'S GREENBELT MOVEMENT
1. When did these movements start?		
2. What do the people who work for these movements want to save? (What is in danger?)		
3. Why are these places in danger?		
4. How are the people trying to save these places?		
5. What are the benefits of the greenbelts?		

1. Look at item 5. Can you think of any other benefits a greenbelt might have, perhaps in another country or another urban area?
2. What will happen in Kenya, San Francisco, and other places if greenbelts disappear?
3. What else can people do to help save nature areas and greenbelts?

5 REVIEWING LANGUAGE

A. EXPLORING LANGUAGE

Two of the three items following each phrase correctly completes the sentence. Cross out the item that does not make sense. The first one has been done for you.

1. Most of the income Norman gets from his farm is from
   a. selling milk.
   b. renting land to other farmers.
   c. ~~buying new equipment~~.
2. My favorite place to go camping is
   a. Los Angeles.
   b. Mount Shasta.
   c. Yellowstone National Park.
3. Builders try to convince towns to let them build more buildings by saying
   a. "The open land here is beautiful."
   b. "We will pay you a lot of money for the land."
   c. "You need more houses in this area."
4. In deserts, you can usually find
   a. sunshine.
   b. trees.
   c. snakes.
5. Bill and his brother, Jay, live in separate places because
   a. Bill prefers the city, while Jay prefers the suburbs.
   b. they love to see each other every day.
   c. they had a big fight and don't talk to each other anymore.
6. One of the benefits of living in a city is
   a. it's noisy.
   b. you can usually live close to shops.
   c. you don't need a car because there are lots of buses.
7. Robert is a member of
   a. my friends.
   b. The Open Space Trust Organization.
   c. a bicycling club.
8. Redwood City just bought 40 acres of
   a. land.
   b. forest.
   c. roads.

B. WORKING WITH WORDS

Complete the following sentences with the words below.

acres	convince	includes	separate
benefits	disappear	members	suburbs
camping	greenbelt	open land	urban

Pauline lives in the (1) ______________ . "You can't (2) ______________ me that the city is better than the suburbs!" she says. "There are a lot of (3) ______________ to living in the suburbs. For example, it is much quieter than the city, and I can have a bigger house here, so the children can all have (4) ______________ bedrooms. My family and I are all (5) ______________ of the swim and tennis club, so there is lots to do on the weekends."

Mark is a farmer near the San Francisco Bay Area. His farm is in the (6) ______________ . "I am really glad the we have a greenbelt because my farm (7) ______________ only 200 (8) ______________ of land," Mark says. "With the greenbelt, I know that the forest around my farm won't (9) ______________ . It would be different if there were cities all around my farm. I wouldn't like it, and I don't think my cows would like it either!"

Warren and Diana live in San Francisco with their two children. They like living in a(n) (10) ______________ area. "We have a car but we almost never have to drive," Diana says. "We can walk to the shops, and we take buses to get to work. Sure, it gets noisy and crowded here sometimes. That's why we go (11) ______________ and walking a lot on the weekends. There are great trails and campgrounds in the (12) ______________ only half an hour away from here."

6 SKILLS FOR EXPRESSION

A. GRAMMAR: Simple Past

❶ *Look at the following sentences. Underline the verbs that tell about something that happened in the past. Underline those in negative statements, too. Then answer the questions that follow.*

In the United States, before the 1940s most people lived in cities and towns, or on farms. If they weren't farmers, they built their houses close to town centers because they wanted to be near shops, schools, and jobs. But, in the 1940s, more people started to buy cars. With cars, people traveled everywhere easily, so they didn't need to live close to city or town centers anymore. People who worked in cities moved out of the cities to nearby areas. Suburbs began to grow.

1. How is the simple past formed?
2. How is the simple past formed in negative statements?

FOCUS ON GRAMMAR

See Simple Past Tense in Statements in *Focus on Grammar, Basic.*

Simple Past

When we talk about things that happened in the past, we use the **simple past tense**.

1. To form the simple past tense for regular verbs, add *-ed* to the base form of the verb.

Base Form of Verb	Simple Past Form
want	want**ed**
work	work**ed**

If the verb ends in *e*, add only *-d*.

Base Form of Verb	Simple Past Form
live	live**d**
arrive	arrive**d**

If the verb ends in *y*, change the *y* to *i* and then add *-ed*.

Base Form of Verb	Simple Past Form
study	stud**ied**
try	tr**ied**

2. Many verbs have irregular past tense forms. Here are some of these irregular verbs:

Base Form of Verb	Simple Past Form
be	was / were
build	built
find	found
grow	grew
make	made
teach	taught

3. In negative statements, use *didn't* (*did not*) + base form of the verb, except with the verb *be*:

Base Form of Verb	Simple Past Form
be	wasn't / weren't
need	didn't need
want	didn't want

2 *Complete the paragraphs with the past tense forms of the verbs provided. Some of the verbs are regular and some are irregular.*

Greenbelt Alliance has done many things to help save the Bay Area's greenbelt. Here are some examples of things it did between 1991 and 1996. During those five years, Greenbelt Alliance ________________ (1. help) to save more than 600,000 acres of greenbelt land. It ________________ (2. work) with many other groups and ________________ (3. teach) people why it is important to save some open land. The Alliance ________________ (4. start) new organizations to buy pieces of open land. Greenbelt Alliance ________________ (5. convince) city and state governments to make laws that stop new building on open land. Volunteers also ________________ (6. take) people on walks to show them the beautiful natural areas nearby.

Greenbelt Alliance ________________ (7. not try) to stop all new building in the Bay Area between 1991 and 1996. It only ________________ (8. try) to get builders to build near town centers and transportation.

❸ *Look at the maps of the San Francisco Bay Area from 1900, 1940, and 1990. Read the sentences. Use the phrases to write sentences in the past tense. The first one has been done for you.*

1900

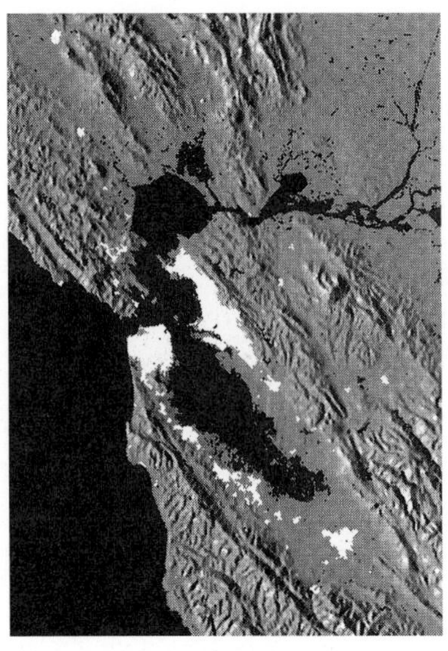

1940

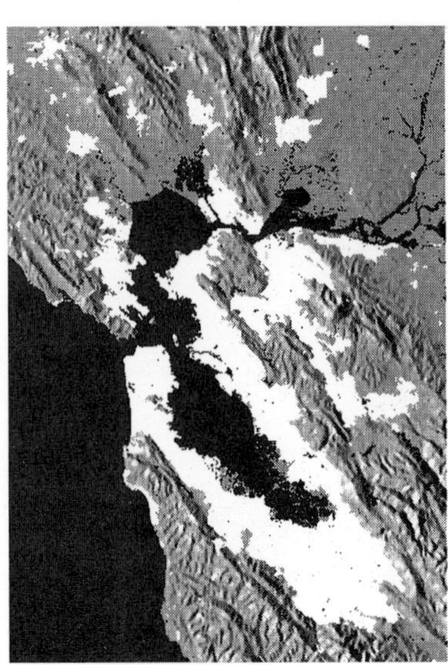

1990

1. Now there is a lot of suburban sprawl in the San Francisco Bay Area.
   In 1900, there wasn't a lot of suburban sprawl.
2. Now the towns touch each other.
   In 1940, ______________________________.
3. Now the towns aren't separate.
   Before, ______________________________.
4. The urban and suburban area didn't grow a lot between 1900 and 1940.
   ______________________________ between 1940 and 1990.
5. Now cities and suburban sprawl cover a lot of the flat area.
   In 1940, ______________________________.
6. Now the Bay Area has many people.
   In 1940, ______________________________.

B. STYLE: Punctuation

1 *Reread the following section of the brochure from Reading One. Circle all of the punctuation (periods, commas, etc.). Then answer the questions that follow.*

How big is the Greenbelt?
The Greenbelt includes about 3.75 million of the Bay Area's 4.5 million acres. The other 731,000 acres are urban or suburban. San Francisco, for example, covers 30,000 acres; Santa Rosa covers 22,000 acres; San Jose covers more than 100,000 acres.

What is the "open land" in the Greenbelt?
Open land is land that has few buildings and lots of natural areas. The Greenbelt's open land includes parks, forests, beaches, and more than 8,500 farms.

What are the benefits of the Greenbelt?
The Greenbelt has many benefits for people in the Bay Area, which include:

- walking, camping, and biking areas close to the cities and towns
- places for wild plants and animals
- cleaner air and water
- separate towns (it stops towns from growing together)
- income from farms.

How many different kinds of punctuation did you find?

What is each kind of punctuation used for?

Punctuation

. period

Use a period to end a sentence that is a statement.

◆ Open land is land that has few buildings and lots of natural areas.

When you use a period as part of a number, call it "point."

◆ The Greenbelt includes **3.75** ("three point seven five") million of the Bay Area's **4.5** ("four point five") million acres.

$3.75 = 3\frac{3}{4}$ $4.5 = 4\frac{1}{2}$

, comma

Commas are used for many different reasons, usually to separate parts of a sentence. One of the most common uses is to separate short items in a list.

◆ The Greenbelt's open land includes parks**,** forests**,** beaches**,** and more than 8,500 farms.

We also use commas to help us read numbers that are larger than 999. Commas go in front of every third digit from the right.

◆ San Francisco covers 30**,**000 acres; Santa Rosa covers 22**,**000 acres; San Jose covers more than 100**,**000 acres.

? question mark

Use a question mark to end a question.

◆ How big is the Greenbelt**?**

: colon

A colon sometimes introduces a list, especially if the list has long items.

◆ The Greenbelt has many benefits for people in the Bay Area, which include:

- walking, camping, and biking close to the cities and towns
- places for wild plants and animals

; semicolon

A semicolon can be used instead of a period if two statements are very closely related.

- San Francisco covers 30,000 acres**;** Santa Rosa covers 22,000 acres**;** San Jose covers more than 100,000 acres.

" " quotation marks

Quotation marks are used to report exactly what someone said.

- Joe said, **"**I want to become a member of the Greenbelt Alliance.**"**

Quotation marks are also used around new words or expressions that the reader might not understand.

- What is the **"**open land**"** in the Greenbelt?

' apostrophe

Apostrophes are used to show possession.

- The Greenbelt**'**s open land includes parks, forests, beaches, and more than 8,500 farms.

They are also used in contractions.

- do not = don**'**t
- I am = I**'**m

( ) parentheses

Parentheses can go around information that helps explain something in a sentence but isn't needed to understand the sentence. For example, parentheses can go around definitions, background information, and examples.

- The Greenbelt has many benefits for people in the Bay Area, which include:
  - separate towns **(**it stops towns from growing together**)**. . .

2 *Put the correct punctuation in the blanks.*

1. $3\frac{1}{3}$ = 3___333
2. 300 + 700 = 1___000
3. Where is Kenya ___
4. Kenya is a country in East Africa ___
5. The Kalahari ___ the Sahara ___ and the Chalbi are deserts in Africa.
6. The Sahara is in the north ___ the Kalahari is in the south ___ the Chalbi is in the east.
7. Wangari Maathai has done many things to help make Kenya a better place to live ___
   - She started Kenya's Greenbelt Movement.
   - She stopped a skyscraper from being built in the middle of a park in Nairobi ___ Nairobi is the capital of Kenya ___ .
   - She tries to convince politicians to do things to save Kenya's forests, animals, and people.
8. ___ Deforestation ___ means that the forest is disappearing from an area ___ ___ desertification ___ means that an area is becoming desert.
9. Africa___s deserts are disappearing quickly.

3 *A student wrote the following short paper and got it back from his teacher with comments. Rewrite the short paper. Correct the punctuation.*

Youssef Outouda

When I was a child in Morocco, I spent a lot of time in nature because my town was in an oasis. The oasis is 15,5 km long, so we could go for long walks. My favorite place to go was the river at the end of the oasis. My friends and I used to go swimming have picnics play soccer and study there. Old women sometimes went there to pick herbs and shepherds brought their sheep there for water and young women sometimes went there to wash their clothes. Have you ever been to Morocco I hope you'll be able to go one day

An oasis?! How wonderful!

What is this number?

Separate items in a list

Too many ands—can you separate these statements?

Don't forget punctuation here

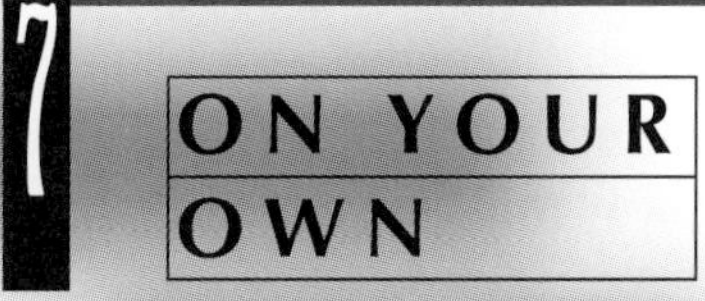

A. WRITING TOPICS

Choose one of the following topics. Write one or two paragraphs. Use some of the vocabulary, grammar, and style that you learned in this unit.

1. Write about a day that you spent in nature. Where did you go? What did you do? Did you enjoy it? Why or why not?

2. Do you prefer to live in an urban, a suburban, or a rural (country) area? Why? What are the benefits of the area you prefer?

3. Write about an area you know that you remember as open land but that became part of a suburb or town. What was it like before? What is it like now? Do you think it was a good idea to build on that land? Why or why not?

B. FIELDWORK

Find out how the area you live in now (your neighborhood or your town or city) has changed over the years.

1. Find someone who has lived in your area for a long time. You might try people in your apartment building, at your school, or at your job. You might even try going to a retirement home to see if you can find someone to talk to there. Make an appointment to interview that person.

2. Make a list of questions about your area. You might ask the following:

   How was __________ different from the way it is now?

   When was __________ built?

   Was there more nature and open land before? Where was it?

3. At your interview take notes. You might want to bring a map to help the person you interview explain things. You also might want to record the conversation and take notes later. (If you want to tape the conversation, first ask the person you are interviewing if it's OK.)

4. From your notes, write a description of your area during this earlier period. You might want to draw maps to show the changes.

5. Make a short oral presentation to your class. Use maps to show your classmates the places you describe.

UNIT 3

MAKING MONEY

U.S. $100 bill before 1996

U.S. $100 bill after 1996

1 APPROACHING THE TOPIC

A. PREDICTING

Look at the bills. Discuss your answers to the questions.
1. Why do you think the $100 bill was changed?
2. What differences can you see between the two bills?

B. SHARING INFORMATION

What do you think about the following actions? Are they acceptable? Are they wrong? Some things may seem more wrong to you than others. For each action, check (√) the box that shows what you think. Compare your answers in small groups.

VERY WRONG 1	WRONG 2	NOT SO WRONG 3	ACCEPTABLE 4	
				a. A student doesn't want to buy a book he needs, so he copies some chapters on a copy machine.
				b. A student copies a friend's paper and gives it to her teacher with her own name on it.
				c. A man finds a purse with $500 in it. He keeps the money.
				d. A man needs some money. He copies paper money on a copy machine.
				e. A woman needs some money. She takes $50 from her mother's wallet.

2 PREPARING TO READ

A. BACKGROUND

When you read a story, there may be many words you don't know. Often you can still understand the story, and sometimes you can even understand these new words.

Read the following story. See if you can understand it even though some words are missing. Answer the questions that follow. Discuss your answers with a classmate.

One day in 1993 some New York City garbage workers were very surprised when they emptied a trash can. Along with the banana peels and empty Coke cans, they found $18 million in new (1) ______________.

Who would throw out all that money? The workers felt that something was not right, so they called the United States Bureau of Engraving and Printing, the department that makes paper money. The government workers said that the money looked real but that it was actually (2) ______________—and not legal. The garbage belonged to (3) ______________, people who make money that is not real. They make the money by using (4) ______________ similar to those for making books or newspapers or by using (5) ______________ and other computer equipment. These counterfeiters probably made a lot of money and weren't happy with how it looked. So they threw it out and made some more.

1. What did the New York garbage workers find?

____

2. Who threw out all that money?

____

B. VOCABULARY FOR COMPREHENSION

Read the story again. With a partner, use information in the story to guess the meaning of the missing words. Write your guesses on the lines that follow.

1. ____
2. ____
3. ____
4. ____
5. ____
6. ____

Now read the story with the vocabulary words filled in.

One day in 1993 some New York City garbage workers were very surprised when they emptied a trash can. Along with the banana peels and empty Coke cans, they found $18 million in new (1) <u>bills</u>.

Who would throw out all that money? The workers felt that something was not right, so they called the United States Bureau of Engraving and Printing, the department that makes paper money. The government workers said that the money looked real but that it was actually (2) <u>fake</u>—and not legal. The garbage belonged to (3) <u>counterfeiters</u>, people who make money that is not real. They make the money by using (4) <u>printing presses</u> similar to those for making books or newspapers or by using (5) <u>scanners</u> and other computer equipment. These counterfeiters probably made a lot of money and weren't happy with how it looked. So they threw it out and made some more.

*As a class, compare your definitions. Together write one definition that seems **best** for each word.*

3

READING ONE: Making Money

A. INTRODUCING THE TOPIC

The following article is about how counterfeiters make fake money. It is also about how the U.S. government tries to stop counterfeiting. In groups of three, make a list of things that you think the government might do to make money harder to copy.

____

____

____

____

____

____

Making Money

1 It was so quick and easy. A fourteen-year-old boy in Scottsdale, Arizona, pulled out his \$50 bill and put it onto his school's new computer scanner. Then he printed ten copies of his \$50 bill on a color copier. Within seconds he changed \$50 into \$550, and he was ready to shop.

2 Twenty years ago only a few people had the skills or equipment to make counterfeit money. Today computer, copier, and printer technology is so good that almost anyone can "make" money. With the new technology there is a new kind of counterfeiter: *casual counterfeiters*. These counterfeiters are called *casual* because they don't have special skills and because they don't need to plan much.

3 The number of bills made by casual counterfeiters on their home or office computer is growing fast. In fact, this number has doubled every year since 1989! There is no way to stop counterfeiting 100 percent. But the government has recently found a few ways to make casual counterfeiting very difficult.

4 One way is to put very, very small words, called *microprint,* in hidden places on the bill. These words are only $\frac{6}{1000}$ inch. No one can read them without a magnifying glass, a special glass that makes things look bigger. And they are too small to come out clearly on a copier. If someone copies a bill that has microprint and you look at the copy through

a magnifying glass, instead of microprinted words, you will see only black lines.

5 Another way to stop people from making counterfeit money on their home computers is to use special color-changing ink. Money printed with color-changing ink will look green from one angle and yellow from another. Home computers cannot use color-changing ink. So any copies from a home computer will have normal ink and can be noticed quite easily.

6 Additionally, money is made on special paper with very small pieces of red and blue silk mixed in. And on each bill there is a special line that runs from the top to the bottom of the bill. Suppose, for example, that you hold a $20 bill up to the light. If you do this, you can see the line has the words "USA twenty." The line turns red if you put it under a special (ultraviolet) light. This line and the special paper with red and blue silk are not easy for home computers to copy.

7 The government must try many different ways to stop counterfeiting. The Bureau of Engraving and Printing needs to keep changing the way money is made because counterfeiters can learn to copy the changes. Today copiers can't copy microprinted words or color-changing ink. But, in a few years, who knows?

B. READING FOR MAIN IDEAS

1 *The following sentences tell the main ideas of the seven paragraphs in "Making Money." Read the sentences. For each, write the correct paragraph number. The first one has been done for you.*

	Paragraph
a. Casual counterfeiting is becoming a big problem, and the government is fighting the problem.	3
b. Color-changing ink is a way to stop counterfeiters.	______
c. A child can easily copy paper money.	______
d. The government must always keep changing the bills to stop people from counterfeiting.	______
e. Microprint is a way to stop counterfeiters.	______
f. New technology makes casual counterfeiting possible.	______
g. Special paper and a special line are two ways to stop counterfeiters.	______

2 *Check (√) the sentence that* **best** *describes the main idea of the whole article.*

____ **a.** It's easier to counterfeit money today than it was twenty years ago.

____ **b.** The government has several ways to try to stop counterfeiters.

____ **c.** New technology makes counterfeiting easier, but the government has changed bills to make counterfeiting more difficult.

C. READING FOR DETAILS

Complete the sentences with information from the text.

1. Twenty years ago, only a few people had the ________ or ________ to make fake money.
2. One way to stop counterfeiters from making fake money on a ________ is to use microprinted words.
3. Bills have a ________ that you can see if you hold them up to the light.
4. Bills are printed on special paper that has pieces of __________ and ________ silk.
5. A boy in Scottsdale, Arizona, used his school's scanner to make ________ copies of a $ ________ bill.
6. Money printed with color-changing ink looks green from one angle and ________ from another.

D. READING BETWEEN THE LINES

Based on the information in the text, which of the following statements do you think are true? Write **T** *for true,* **F** *for false. While some answers may be better than others, there aren't right or wrong answers. Compare your answers with a partner, and discuss the reasons for your answers.*

____ **1.** Some casual counterfeiters counterfeit a lot of money, but others counterfeit only a few bills.

____ **2.** Casual counterfeiters are bad people.

____ **3.** Casual counterfeiters are easy to catch.

____ **4.** Today most counterfeit money is made by casual counterfeiters.

____ **5.** The government changes the way it makes money every few years.

____ **6.** Copiers will be able to copy microprint in just a few years.

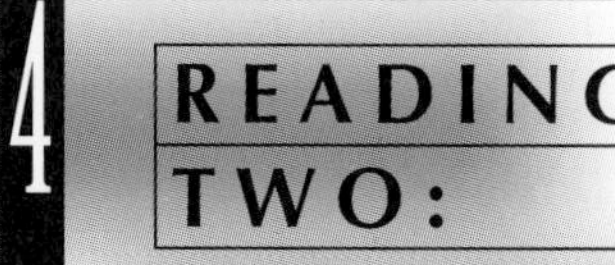

4 READING TWO: I Made It Myself

A. EXPANDING THE TOPIC

Before computers and copiers, counterfeiting was not easy. You needed a large printing press, the skill to use the press, and the artistic skill to copy a bill. Counterfeiting often took a lot of time, planning, and hard work. But the results were excellent. The counterfeit money looked and felt like the real thing. Today, professional counterfeiters still make fake money the old way—on printing presses.

Read the story of Michael Landress, who was once a professional counterfeiter. Then answer the questions that follow. Check your answers with a partner.

I Made It Myself

1 It took months of planning, of trying to find the perfect paper, of mixing and remixing ink to get the right color, of printing and reprinting to get the right feel, but I did it. I made a perfect copy of a $100 bill.

2 During the days, I did regular print jobs at the shop. Then every evening at five o'clock, I sent my workers home, hoping no one would ask why I stayed late. I pulled out the paper, ink, and other equipment I hid away the night before and slowly, carefully worked until the sun came up. I didn't have time to sleep. I was too nervous to sleep anyway. As I worked, I worried about the Secret Service[1] men coming to get me. In the beginning, as I prepared the paper, I said to myself, "I'm just printing little blue and red hair lines on paper. They can't arrest me for that." Then as I printed the numbers, I said, "I'm just printing small numbers in four corners of a page. They can't arrest me for *this*." Finally, as I got closer and closer to printing something I could be arrested for, I began to wonder, "Is this really that bad? Who am I hurting? I'm making myself a few thousand dollars so I can take my boy and move to Puerto Rico. I'm just trying to do my best for my family. Is that so wrong?"

---

[1] The Secret Service is the government agency that tries to find and catch counterfeiters.

3 After about three weeks of slow work, I finally printed out a whole sheet of $100 bills. I took out the magnifying glass and studied my work. "No. Oh, Ben, no. Ben, you don't look right," I said aloud to the empty shop. The portrait of Ben Franklin on the front of the bill just didn't look right. To most people, he probably looked like the one on the real bill. But I could see that it wasn't a perfect copy. I needed it to be perfect. So, slowly, painfully I started over.

4 A week later, I was printing the last of the bills. I didn't hear them come in because of the noise of the press. I just looked up from studying the now-perfect portraits of Ben Franklin to see a gun at my head and hear the Secret Service man say, "Just like getting caught with your hand in the cookie jar, huh, Mike?"

Adapted from M. M. Landress with Bruce Dobler. *I Made It Myself* (New York: Grosset and Dunlap, 1973).

1. The title of the story is "I Made It Myself." What does "it" refer to?

2. In the third paragraph, Landress says, "No. Oh, Ben, no." Who is Ben? What was wrong?

3. In the fourth paragraph, Landress says, "I didn't hear them come in because of the noise of the press." Who does "them" refer to?

4. The story ends with "Just like getting caught with your hand in the cookie jar, huh, Mike?" What do you think "getting caught with your hand in the cookie jar" means?

B. LINKING READINGS ONE AND TWO

There are two kinds of counterfeiters: casual counterfeiters, like the fourteen-year-old boy in Scottsdale, Arizona, and professional counterfeiters like Mike Landress. Based on the readings, compare the two kinds of counterfeiters. Put checks (√) in the boxes on page 50. Explain your answers to your classmates.

	CASUAL COUNTERFEITERS	PROFESSIONAL COUNTERFEITERS
1. make fake money more quickly		
2. make better-looking fake money		
3. won't be affected by microprint		
4. make fake money that really feels like real money		
5. need special skills		
6. do much more counterfeiting than they did twenty years ago		
7. can get caught more easily		

REVIEWING LANGUAGE

A. EXPLORING LANGUAGE

Write each vocabulary word in the box(es) of the workplace(s) where people are likely to use the word. The words can go in several boxes. Different answers are possible. Be prepared to explain your answers.

bill

counterfeit

ink

magnifying glass

portrait

press

scanner

thief

Northampton Police Department
The *Star Daily*

Joe's Photography Lab

"We use high-tech equipment to give you the photograph *you* want."

Kwik Kopy

"Let us make all your copies—black and white or color."

Bureau of Engraving and Printing

B. WORKING WITH WORDS

Complete the sentences with the words in the list below.

bill	equipment	portrait	skill
casual	fake	scanner	

1. Printing presses, copiers, scanners, ink, and magnifying glasses are different kinds of ________________ used in counterfeiting.
2. The artist painted a(n) ________________ of each president.
3. Everyone liked the artist's work and thought it showed great ________________.
4. I want to be able to put this photograph on my computer screen. I need a(n) ________________.
5. Don't be fooled by that "Rolex" watch. It's cheap because it's a(n) ________________.
6. I need change. Can I have four quarters for a one-dollar ________________?
7. He's very ________________ about his business—I don't think he takes it at all seriously.

A. GRAMMAR: Comparisons with Adjectives

❶ *Read the following advertisement. Underline all the words that end in* **-er**. *Then answer the questions that follow.*

COUNTERFEIT MONEY DETECTOR

Protect your business against counterfeit money!

Our new machine for checking bills is faster than the old machines. And our machine is easier to use than the old machines. All you do is put a bill in the machine. If the bill is counterfeit, an alarm bell will ring. It's as easy as that! Counterfeit protection is here. Buy the ***Counterfeit Money Detector*** today and you can sleep well tonight.

You have to be smarter than the counterfeiters! Buy our machine.

Counterfeit Money Detector—$450
Call today. Call 1-800-23-MONEY

1. What three words did you underline?

______________ ______________ ______________

2. What word follows each of these words? ______________________

FOCUS ON GRAMMAR

See Comparative Forms of Adjectives in *Focus on Grammar, Basic.*

Comparative Form of Adjectives

The words you underlined are adjectives in the comparative form. Use the **comparative form of adjectives** to compare two people, places, or things.	Our new machine is **faster** than the old machine. You have to be **smarter** than the counterfeiters.
If the adjective has one syllable, add *-er* to make the comparative. Add only *-r* if the word ends in *e*.	fast → fast**er** old → old**er** large → large**r**

For most adjectives that have two or more syllables, add *more* before the adjective to make the comparative.	In the past it was **more difficult** than it is today to counterfeit money.
If a two-syllable adjective ends in *-y*, change *y* to *i* and add *-er*.	Today it is **easier** than in the past to counterfeit money.
Use *than* after the comparative form and before the second person, place, or thing.	This machine is easier to use **than** the old one. Dixon is faster **than** Amy.
If the second person, place, or thing is understood, do not use *than*.	Bart doesn't like his bicycle. He wants to buy one that is faster.
Don't forget the exceptions:	good → better bad → worse

2 *David and Will are two high school students. Today they feel bored in class, so they are passing notes back and forth. Read the notes. Complete the notes with the comparative form of the adjective provided. The first one has been done for you.*

Dave,

Can you believe how boring this class is? Argh! This is even

<u>more boring</u> than Shoemaker's history class!
1. boring

Will

Yeah. I'm almost asleep over here. Did you hear what Tom did last weekend? Wow. It's __________ (2. bad) ***than anything I've ever done.***

No. What?

You know that old car of his? He really wanted to buy a ________ (3. good) ***one. But he didn't have any money. So guess what he did?***

He stole money from his parents?

No, he did something much _______________ than
4. crazy
that! He copied a $100 bill on his family's new scanner and printed it out with their color printer.

Wow! Doesn't he know counterfeiting is illegal?

I know. I told him. But he said he's ___________ than
5. smart
most car salesmen. He says they won't even know the money is fake.

This is _______________ than anything he's ever done. He could
6. dangerous
go to jail!

I know. I told him all that, too. He just said making money this way is ____________ and ____________ than
7. easy 8. fast
getting a job. Can you believe it?

Tom's crazy! He's really going too far this time!

3 *Write sentences comparing these two anticounterfeit machines. Use the adjectives in the following list to help you. The first one has been done for you.*

bad	easy (to use)	good	small
cheap	expensive	large	~~strong~~
difficult (to use)	fast	slow	

ELECTRONIC CASH SCANNER	CURRENCY VALIDATOR PEN

$525	$19.95
will last for ten years To use: Place bills in machine and wait for machine to electronically scan them.	will test up to 5,000 bills To use: Make a small dot on each bill with the pen. Wait for the color to turn dark brown (counterfeit) or to turn yellow (good).
If bills are counterfeit, a red light flashes and an alarm sounds.	If bills are counterfeit, a dark spot appears on bill.

1. The Electronic Cash Scanner is stronger than the Currency Validator Pen.
2. __________
3. __________
4. __________
5. __________
6. __________
7. __________
8. __________
9. __________
10. __________
11. __________

B. STYLE: Transition Words of Addition and Contrast

1 *Read the paragraph and answer the questions that follow.*

Small-time thieves have a couple ways to make counterfeit money quickly. For example, they cut off the numbers from the four corners of a $20 bill and glue them onto the corner of four $1 bills. (1) Also, they copy a $50 bill on a color copier and try to use the copy as real money. (2) However, these people are easy to catch. Only professional counterfeiters can make bills that look real.

a. Which underlined sentence adds information that is similar to information in the sentence before it? ______________________

b. Which underlined sentence adds information that is different from information in the sentence before it? ______________________

Transition Words

Transition words of addition and contrast help you connect sentences when you compare two things.

Transition words of addition connect two sentences that have similar ideas. These transitions include *in addition, additionally, also,* and *too.*

Transition words of contrast connect two sentences that have opposite ideas. These transitions include *however* and *in contrast.*

Transition words usually come at the beginning of the sentence. But, the transition word *too* always comes at the end of the sentence. Put a comma after a transition word at the beginning of a sentence; put a comma before the transition *too.*

- American dollar bills have microprinted words. **In addition,** they have color-changing ink. They have special paper**, too.**

2 *Read the paragraphs. Complete the paragraphs with the transition words of addition and contrast listed below. You may use the transition words several times. In most blanks, more than one transition word is correct.*

also   however   in addition   in contrast   too

There have been many changes made to the U.S. $100 bill. The portrait has changed. The ink has changed, (1) ______________. (2) ______________, the size and color of the bills have not changed.

The new $100 bill has a larger portrait of Ben Franklin. This picture is easier to see, and the added detail is harder to copy. (3) ______________, the portrait is now off center to make room for a watermark[1] and to prevent the portrait from getting wrinkled.

The ink has been changed from a single-color ink to a color-shifting ink. This ink will appear green from one angle and yellow from another.

These changes help make the bills difficult to copy. (4) ______________, some things have not changed. For example, the bill is still 6 inches by $2\frac{1}{2}$ inches. The paper is still a cotton/linen mix. (5) ______________, the colors remain black on the front of the bill and green on the back. (6) ______________, because of the color-shifting ink, the green does change a little when you look at it from a different angle.

3 *Use your understanding of transitions to put these sentences into the correct order.*

____ Also, you can run your hand over the bill. Sometimes people glue higher numbers onto $1 bills. You can easily feel these bills right away.

____ Sometimes it's easy to tell if your money is counterfeit. You can look at the microprinted words under a magnifying glass. If you can read them, your money should be real.

____ On the other hand, it's sometimes very difficult to tell if money is counterfeit. If a professional made the counterfeit, you won't feel anything unusual and you might be able to read the microprinted words.

---

[1] Watermark: a design put into paper that can only be seen when held up to the light

4 *Suppose that you work in a store and that your boss has asked you to choose an anticounterfeiting device for the store. You have decided the store should buy the cash scanner.*

Look back at exercise 3 in Section 6A on page 54–55. Find one sentence you wrote that gives a reason why the pen is better. Find three sentences that give reasons why the scanner is better. Use these sentences and three transition words to complete the note.

I looked at the Currency Validator Pen and the Electronic Cash Scanner.

I think we should buy the Electronic Cash Scanner for our store.

____

____

____

____

____

____

____

____

____

7 ON YOUR OWN

A. WRITING TOPICS

Choose one of the following topics. Write one or two paragraphs. Use some of the vocabulary, grammar, and style that you learned in this unit.

1. Compare casual counterfeiters to professional counterfeiters. Use the information from the readings and from the exercises.

2. The word *counterfeit* applies to anything fake. For example, you can buy counterfeit Levi jeans, counterfeit music CDs, or counterfeit computer software.

   Making counterfeit computer software is a serious crime. People copy expensive software and then sell it for less than it costs in the stores. Compare counterfeiting computer software to counterfeiting money. Which one is more difficult? Which one is a worse crime? Explain.

B. FIELDWORK

Find out about how banks look for counterfeit money and about what they do when they see it. To get this information, your class will write letters to several banks. Follow these steps:

1. In small groups, make a list of five or more questions you want to ask. Questions might include the following:

   Do you check your bills to see if they are counterfeit? If so, how?

   How often do you catch counterfeit money?

   What do you do if you know someone is giving you counterfeit money?

   ____

   ____

   ____

   ____

   ____

   ____

2. In pairs, write your letter in correct business letter format (see Unit 4, Section 6B, pages 75–76). In the letter, follow these steps:

   a. Address the letter to the Bank Branch Manager.

   b. Introduce yourselves. Explain that you are writing this letter for a class assignment and that you want to find out about the bank's counterfeiting policies.

   c. Ask your questions about the counterfeiting policies.

   d. Give your teacher's name and the school's mailing address so someone at the bank can send you an answer.

   e. Thank the branch manager for taking the time to read your letter and answer you.

3. Choose several different banks to send the letters to. The banks can be local—or can even be in other countries.

UNIT 4

SAVE THE ELEPHANTS

1 APPROACHING THE TOPIC

A. PREDICTING

Look at the picture. Discuss your answers to the questions.

1. **Which animals do you know?**
2. **Which of these animals have you seen only in pictures?**
3. **Which of these animals have you actually seen? Where did you see them?**

B. SHARING INFORMATION

Some of these animals are extinct (not alive anymore). Some are endangered (only a small number are still alive). And some are not in any danger. In small groups, share what you know about the animals. Try to put each animal in the correct list.

EXTINCT	ENDANGERED	NOT IN DANGER

2 PREPARING TO READ

A. BACKGROUND

Read the three Web pages on pages 63–64. Discuss the questions that follow.

Friends of the Tiger

Go To: http://www.save.the.tiger

One hundred years ago there were 100,000 wild tigers in the world. Today there are only 5,000 tigers. Hunters kill many tigers. Other tigers die because people cut down their forests to make room for houses. Friends of the Tiger wants to stop hunters and protect forests.

Call 1-800-5-TIGERS for more information.

Page 1 of 1

Save the Northern Spotted Owl

Go To: http://www.save.the.owl

Every year there are 4% fewer northern spotted owls in the forests of the Pacific Northwest of America. Today only 3,600 remain. Logging companies have been cutting down the redwood trees for wood. These trees are the owls' homes. Help us stop the logging companies.

Call 1-800-SAVEOWL.

Page 1 of 1

The Panda Project

Go To: http://www.save.the.panda

Three hundred years ago there were hundreds of thousands of wild pandas in China. Today there are only 1,000. Pandas eat bamboo[1]. But bamboo forests grow smaller every year as people cut down the bamboo trees to make room for houses. The Panda Project wants to protect the pandas' home.

Call 1-800-4-PANDAS to learn how you can help.

[1] *bamboo*: a woody plant that grows in China

Page 1 of 1

1. Why are these animals endangered? ______________________

____

____

2. What are Friends of the Tiger and the other groups trying to do?

____

____

____

3. Do you think it is important to save endangered animals? Why or why not? ______________________

____

____

B. VOCABULARY FOR COMPREHENSION

Read the sentences in the box. Then read the sentences that follow. On the line following each of these sentences, write the correct sentence from the box. The first one has been done for you. (There are two answers for item 7).

These people are guards.	They are called tusks.
They are endangered.	They protect the animals.
These people are hunters.	They are native to Africa.
It is made from ivory.	~~They are extinct~~.

1. There were lots of dinosaurs many years ago, but now there are none.
They are extinct.

2. There used to be many elephants in Africa. Now there are very few. Soon there might be none. __________

3. Elephants have lived in Africa for many, many years.

____

4. Some people kill animals. __________

5. An elephant has two very long white "teeth" on its face.

____

6. I have a beautiful bracelet. It is made of elephant tusks.

____

7. Some people watch the elephant parks so that no one kills the animals.

____

____

3 READING ONE: Save the Elephants

A. INTRODUCING THE TOPIC

Read the title and the first paragraph of the letter. Then answer these questions.

1. Who is the letter to?
2. Who is the letter from?
3. What do you think the writer of the letter wants?

SAVE THE ELEPHANTS FUND
2354 MASSACHUSETTS AVENUE, NW
WASHINGTON, D.C. 01012

October 14

Dear Friend of SAVE THE ELEPHANTS FUND,

1 Thank you for your donation of $25 last year. Your money helped us to open a new elephant park in Kenya as part of our effort to help protect the 500,000 elephants left in Africa.

2 But elephants are endangered in other parts of the world, too, and we need your help again. This time we need you to help us in Thailand.

3 One hundred years ago, 100,000 wild elephants lived in Asia. Today there are only 30,000 Asian elephants. The situation in Thailand is especially serious. Thailand now has only 1,800–2,000 elephants. Experts believe that by the year 2010, elephants in Thailand will be extinct.

4 *Why are elephants in Thailand endangered?*

5 ◆ They don't have enough food to eat.
Paper companies cut down banana trees and bamboo. These plants are native to Thailand, and they provide elephants with food. The companies plant eucalyptus trees instead. The eucalyptus trees grow fast and provide the companies with wood for boxes and other paper products. The paper companies make a lot of money from the eucalyptus trees. But what about the elephants? They can't eat eucalyptus trees!

6 ◆ Hunters kill hundreds of wild elephants every year.
Hunting elephants is not legal in Thailand. But Thailand has poachers, hunters who kill animals even though it is not legal. These poachers make a lot of money from selling elephant tusks. The only way to get the tusk off the elephant is to kill the animal. The poachers sell the tusks to people who make furniture, jewelry, and art from the ivory in the tusks.

7 *What can we do?*

8 With your help and donation, this year we will:

- teach companies in Thailand about trees that are good for business and good for elephants.
- pay for guards to protect the elephants from poachers.
- convince people around the world not to buy things made of ivory.
- help poachers to find other ways to make money.

9 Last year you helped Kenya's elephants. This year Thailand's elephants need your help. Please send your donation today.

Thank you.

Sincerely,

Mark Gow

Mark Gow
Executive Director

B. READING FOR MAIN IDEAS

With a partner, answer the following questions.

1. What is the general purpose of Save the Elephants Fund? ____________

   ____

2. Why are elephants in Thailand endangered? ____________

   ____

3. What can Save the Elephants Fund do to help protect elephants in Thailand? ____________

   ____

C. READING FOR DETAILS

*Decide if the sentences are true or false. Write **T** or **F** next to each sentence. Compare answers with your partner.*

____ 1. Last year Save the Elephants Fund used donations to open an elephant park in Kenya.

____ 2. There are more than 2,000 wild elephants in Thailand now.

____ 3. Paper companies in Thailand find banana trees useful for boxes and other paper products.

____ 4. In Thailand, it is not legal to hunt elephants.

____ 5. Save the Elephants Fund wants the paper companies to leave Thailand.

____ 6. Save the Elephants Fund wants to help poachers in Thailand to find other jobs.

D. READING BETWEEN THE LINES

Answer the questions. Check your answers with a classmate.

1. Does the writer of the letter know the reader? How do you know?

   ____

   ____

2. The letter says, ". . . we need your help . . ." What does that mean? What kind of help does Save the Elephants Fund want?

   ____

   ____

3. Why does Save the Elephants Fund tell the reader how many elephants there are in Thailand today?

   ____

   ____

4. Save the Elephants Fund says it wants to convince people not to buy ivory. How does this help save elephants?

   ____

   ____

5. Save the Elephants Fund says it will ". . . help poachers find other ways to make money." How does this help save elephants?

   ____

   ____

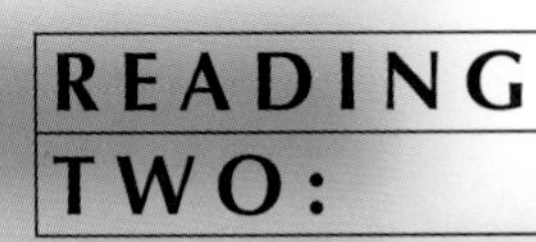

Save a Logger—Eat an Owl

A. EXPANDING THE TOPIC

Read the following letter to the editor of a newspaper. It is a response to an article about the northern spotted owl. Then, in a small group, discuss the questions that follow.

Save a Logger—Eat an Owl

To the Editor:

1 I am really angry about the article on the spotted owl. The article talked only about saving the owl. But what about us—the loggers?

2 The town I live in was built on logging. In the early 1980s, we cut 86 million feet of wood each year. That is a lot of wood. A lot of wood meant a lot of jobs—and a lot of money for the town. This money kept our schools open and our local government running. But by 1992, we were cutting only 100,000 feet of wood a year. Why? Because people like you who just care about the owls stopped us from doing our jobs. You convinced the government to stop logging companies from cutting down so many trees. As a result, over 30,000 logging jobs have been lost. Some people have moved away to find work. Others stayed here and took jobs that pay half of what they made as loggers. People have a hard time putting food on the table for their families. Our schools have no money. Our town is a third of the size that it used to be.

3 I'm not against the spotted owl. But saving the owl is hurting people. What is more important—a few owls or the lives of thousands of hardworking families?

Ken Waxter

1. Why is Ken Waxter angry? ________________________________

2. Why did the logging companies in Ken's town stop cutting down so many trees? ________________________________

3. How does saving the spotted owl hurt Ken Waxter and other people in his town? ________________________________

B. LINKING READINGS ONE AND TWO

In small groups, complete the following chart. Use information from the letters in Readings One and Two. Share your answers with the class.

	ASIAN ELEPHANTS	NORTHERN SPOTTED OWLS
1. Why are the animals endangered?		
2. What can people do to help save these animals?		
3. Who might be hurt by efforts to save the animals? Why?		

Using the information in the chart, discuss these questions with the class.

1. Two different bumper stickers can be seen on cars in the Pacific Northwest: "Save an Owl—Stop Logging," and "Save a Logger—Eat an Owl." How do drivers with each bumper sticker feel about the spotted owl? Why do they feel this way?

2. Why are some animals endangered now? What kinds of things can people do to save them? What kinds of problems happen when people try to save them? Do you think people can save endangered animals **and** avoid these problems? Why or why not?

5

REVIEWING LANGUAGE

A. EXPLORING VOCABULARY

Cross out the word or phrase that is not related to the boldfaced word. The first one has been done for you.

1. **protect:** save, ~~fix~~, guard
2. **wild:** tigers, dogs, whales
3 **donation:** animals, money, help
4. **poacher:** kill, save, illegal
5. **ivory:** white, bird, elephant
6. **tusks:** eucalyptus tree, ivory, elephant
7. **native:** of the place, born in the place, brought into the place
8. **by the year 2010:** between now and the year 2010, before the year 2010, in the year 2010
9. **extinct:** in trouble, gone, dead
10. **endangered:** few, elephants, horses
11. **logger:** animals, trees, worker

B. WORKING WITH WORDS

Look at the following information from Save the Dolphins. Complete the sentences using the words in the list below.

by the year	donation	extinct	protect
convince	endangered	native	

Dear Friend of the Dolphin,

Chinese white dolphins are (1) _____________ to the area near Hong Kong. They are (2) _____________ because the water near Hong Kong is becoming very dirty. If we don't (3) _____________ these dolphins, they might become (4) _____________ (5) _____________ 2020. We need to (6) _____________ companies to stop putting chemicals and garbage in the water. Your (7) _____________ will help us start a Hong Kong Harbor water clean-up project. Please send a check today so that we can save the Chinese white dolphins.

6 SKILLS FOR EXPRESSION

A. GRAMMAR: *Wh-* Questions in the Simple Present Tense

1 *Read the following questions. Look at the verbs in the questions. What is the difference between the verbs in column A and those in column B?*

COLUMN A	COLUMN B
Where *do* elephants *live*?	Who *protects* the elephants in Thailand?
Why *do* poachers *kill* elephants?	What *helps* the elephants?
When *does* Save the Elephants Fund *need* money?	
Who *does* Save the Elephants Fund *need* donations from?	
What *do* elephants *eat*?	

FOCUS ON GRAMMAR

See *Wh-* Questions in the Present Tense in *Focus on Grammar, Basic.*

Wh- Questions in the Simple Present Tense

To form most ***wh-* questions** in the simple present tense, use *do* or *does* and the base form of the verb.

***Wh-* Word**	***Do/Does***	**Subject**	**Base Form of Verb**	
Where	do	elephants	live?	
Why	do	poachers	kill	elephants?
Who	does	Save the Elephants Fund	need	donations from?

Some *wh-* words are *what, where, when, who,* and *why.*

To form *wh-* questions about the subject of a sentence, do not use *do* and *does.* Use the third-person singular form of the verb.

Subject (*Who, What*)	**Third-Person Singular Form of Verb**	
Who	protects	elephants in Thailand?
What	lives	in the park in Kenya?

2 *Read each sentence. Write a question that the underlined words can answer. The first one has been done for you.*

1. Pandas live <u>in China</u>.

   Where do pandas live?

2. <u>Chinese white dolphins</u> live in the water near Hong Kong.

   ____

3. The Chinese white dolphins die <u>because their water is dirty</u>.

   ____

4. Elephants in Thailand like to eat <u>native trees</u>.

   ____

5. Guards protect the elephants <u>in the daytime and at night</u>.

   ____

6. <u>Hunters</u> kill many endangered animals every year.

   ____

3 *Michele works for Save the Elephants Fund, and she is calling Mrs. Jewell. Fill in the missing questions. Use Michele's answers to write the correct questions. The first one has been done for you.*

MRS. JEWELL:	Hello?
MICHELE:	Hi. My name is Michele. I'm calling from the Save the Elephants Fund. Do you have a minute?
MRS. JEWELL:	Sure. Tell me again, (1) who do you work for ?
MICHELE:	I work for Save the Elephants Fund. We try to save endangered elephants in many different countries. This year we're working in Thailand.
MRS. JEWELL:	I thought there were a lot of elephants in Thailand. (2) Why ________________ ?
MICHELE:	We need to save them because they're endangered. There are actually only about 2,000 wild elephants in Thailand now. They're endangered because people kill them and...
MRS. JEWELL:	Oh, no! (3) Who ________________ ?
MICHELE:	Elephant poachers kill them.
MRS. JEWELL:	Really? (4) Why ________________ ?
MICHELE:	Because they want to sell the ivory from the elephants' tusks.
MRS. JEWELL:	That's terrible! What can you do about it? I mean how can I help?
MICHELE:	Well, you can send us a donation.
MRS. JEWELL:	OK. (5) Where ________________ ?
MICHELE:	You send it to 2354 Massachusetts Avenue, NW, Washington, D.C. 01012.
MRS. JEWELL:	(6) Who ________________ ?
MICHELE:	You write the check to "Save the Elephants Fund." Thank you very much for your donation!
MRS. JEWELL:	Oh, you're welcome, and good luck.

B. STYLE: Letter Writing

1 *Letters have five parts: date, opening, body, closing, and signature. Read the letter to Julie from Christine. Try to label the five parts of this letter. The first one has been done for you.*

September 30 — date

Dear Julie,

Hi. How are you? I'm having a great time!

I can't wait to show you the pictures and tell you all about our trip. You know how long I dreamed of going to Africa. I still can't believe it's real. And I really can't believe it's almost over. We have three more days before we fly home. We've seen every animal you can think of. Many of the animals we're seeing are endangered. I feel so lucky to be able to see them. This really is a trip of a lifetime.

I'll call you when we get back in town.

All the best,

Christine

The Five Parts of a Letter

The letter from Christine is a personal letter from one friend to another. Like all letters, it has five parts:

1. **Date:** usually in the top right corner of the paper
2. **Opening:** a greeting to the person you are writing to—"Dear," the person's name, and a comma
3. **Body:** your message—one or more paragraphs
4. **Closing:** a word or phrase (like "All the best," "Best wishes," or "Yours truly") followed by a comma
5. **Signature:** your first name only for people you know; your full name for other people

The letter on page 66 from Save the Elephants Fund is a business letter. A business letter has the same five parts as a personal letter, but there are a few differences.

In a business letter, usually:

- Your name and address come after the date. (The name and address of Save the Elephants Fund comes at the top of the page because it is already printed on the paper. This kind of paper is called letterhead. Most businesses use letterhead when they write letters.)
- If you are writing to a specific person, the name, title, and address of that person comes next, before the opening.
- If you do not know who will read your letter, for the opening write "To Whom It May Concern."
- The closing should be "Sincerely."
- Your name (printed if you are not typing) and job title (if you have one) go under your signature.
- Business letters should be typed if possible.

2 *Label the five parts of the letter from Save the Elephants Fund on page 66.*

3 *Save the Elephants Fund received a large donation from Robin Tucci. Mark Gow must write a letter thanking Robin Tucci for her donation. Write a business letter for him, using the information below. Be sure to include all five parts of a letter.*

To Robin Tucci. Her address is 5325 Sylvan Avenue, Oakland, CA 94618.

From Mark Gow, Executive Director
His address is Save the Elephants Fund
2354 Massachusetts Avenue, NW
Washington, D.C. 01012.

Use today's date.

Message: Thank you for your kind donation of $25. We need all the help we can get. Your money helps us work to save the elephants in Thailand and other parts of the world. Thanks again.

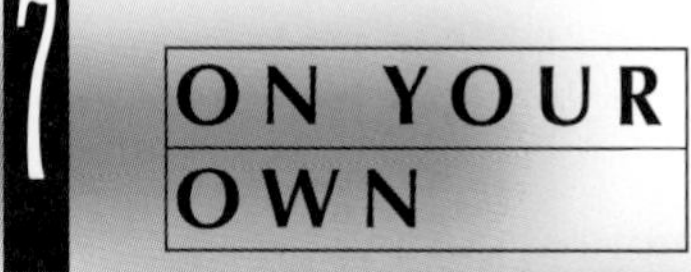

7 ON YOUR OWN

A. WRITING TOPICS

Choose one of the following topics. Write one or two paragraphs. Use some of the vocabulary, grammar, and style that you learned in this unit.

1. You have $300 to donate to one of the groups from Section 2A, pages 62–64, but you have some questions. Write a letter to one of the groups. Say that you want to help but you want to ask some questions first. Ask at least three *wh-* questions. Remember to include all five parts of a letter.

2. You have $300 to donate. Will you give your money to Save the Elephants Fund? Why or why not?

3. Write one or two paragraphs answering the questions in Section 2A, page 64.

4. What are some endangered animals you know about? Do you think it is important to save these and other endangered animals? Why or why not?

B. FIELDWORK

In small groups, write a letter asking for help for an endangered animal.

1. Choose an endangered animal.

2. Get information about this animal from the library or on the Internet. The information should help you answer these questions:

   a. Why is this animal endangered? (at least two reasons)

   b. What can people do to save this animal? (at least two ideas)

   c. What groups (like Save the Elephants Fund or Friends of the Tiger) help protect this animal?

3. Write a letter to the other students in your school, telling them about the endangered animal. In your letter, explain

   a. why this animal is endangered

   b. how they can contact a group to learn more about the problem

   c. how they can help.

Remember to include the parts of a letter. Address the letter to the students in general (e.g., "Dear Fellow Students"), and have everyone in your group sign it.

UNIT 5

SWIMMING ACROSS BORDERS

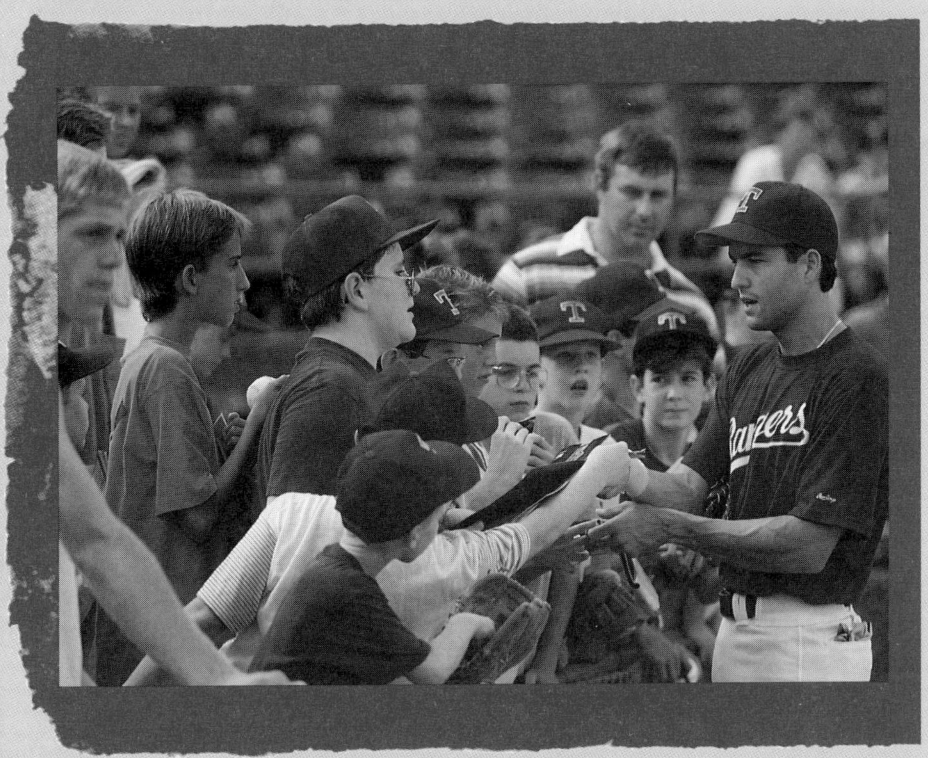

1 APPROACHING THE TOPIC

A. PREDICTING

Look at the picture. Discuss your answers to the questions.

1. Who is the person in the uniform?
2. Who are all the people around him?
3. What are they doing? Why?

B. SHARING INFORMATION

Read the information. Then answer the questions that follow.

Athletes are heroes to us. We admire them, even love them. Why? There are many answers to this question. Consider these major league[1] baseball players:

- Roberto Clemente was among the greatest baseball players of the 1960s. One of the first Latin Americans to play in the major leagues, he helped younger Latin American players. He died in a plane crash while taking food to people in Nicaragua.
- Jim Abbott was born with only part of his right arm. But that didn't stop him from becoming a player. He was on the U.S. Olympic team in 1988 and was also very successful in the major leagues.
- Babe Ruth was one of the greatest baseball players of all time. He had great talent and strength. When he wasn't playing baseball, he was usually out eating, drinking, and having a good time. But people loved him for that, too.
- Ty Cobb was also one of the greatest players. He wasn't the most naturally talented player—or the nicest man. But he worked very hard at baseball, and he treated each game like a war that he had to win.

List three other athletes that you admire.

1. ______________________________
2. ______________________________
3. ______________________________

Why do you admire these athletes? In a small group, use your athletes and the baseball players to discuss different reasons why athletes are heroes to us.

[1] the highest level of professional baseball

2

PREPARING TO READ

A. BACKGROUND

In most sports, athletes can do better if they have certain physical characteristics. For example, tennis player Bjorn Borg has a low heart rate. This helped him to stay strong in long tennis matches.

Can you guess which physical characteristic each athlete has? Why do you think so? Write each letter on a line. Discuss your answers with your class.

____ **1.** Bjorn Borg, tennis player

____ **2.** Carl Lewis, long jumper

____ **3.** Wakanohana Kanzi, sumo wrestler

____ **4.** Wilt Chamberlain, basketball player

____ **5.** Willie Shoemaker, horse-racing jockey

____ **6.** Lynne Cox, cold-water swimmer

a. has an extra layer of fat around heart and other organs

b. weighs 284 pounds (127 kg)

c. is 7'1" tall (216 cm)

d. has a low heart rate

e. is 4'11" tall (150 cm)

f. has extremely long legs

B. VOCABULARY FOR COMPREHENSION

Read the sentences. Circle the letter of the best definition for the underlined word or words.

1. Some people can <u>tolerate</u> hot weather. They can play sports outside on a very hot day and feel fine.

a. not have problems with

b. live in

c. understand

2. In order to be a great athlete, a person needs to both work hard and <u>have talent</u>. Hard work or talent alone is not enough.

   a. be naturally good at something

   b. be able to practice a lot

   c. be interested in learning

3. The runner did more than just win. His time <u>broke the record</u> for the 200-meter race!

   a. was not good enough to win

   b. was good enough to win

   c. was better than the best ever

4. Most athletes are very good at what they do. But every once in a while, an athlete who is truly <u>outstanding</u> comes along and captures the world's attention.

   a. not normal

   b. excellent

   c. better than excellent

5. The <u>border</u> between the United States and Canada stretches from the Atlantic to the Pacific and is the longest border in the world.

   a. distance between two countries

   b. line separating two countries

   c. main road

6. We admire some athletes not only for their <u>achievements</u> as athletes, but also for what they do in other parts of their life.

   a. things that don't work well

   b. things that you do successfully

   c. things that you tell someone

7. She liked the <u>challenge</u> of playing against athletes who were better than she was.

   a. something that is interesting because it is difficult

   b. something that a person does often

   c. something that is easy to do well

3 READING ONE: Swimming to Open Up Borders

A. INTRODUCING THE TOPIC

You will read "Swimming to Open Up Borders," the biography of Lynne Cox, a very special swimmer. Look at the map and the picture. What can you guess about Lynne Cox's life? (Look also at Section 2A, page 81, where Lynne Cox is mentioned.) With a partner, read the following list and check (√) the words you think will be mentioned in the biography.

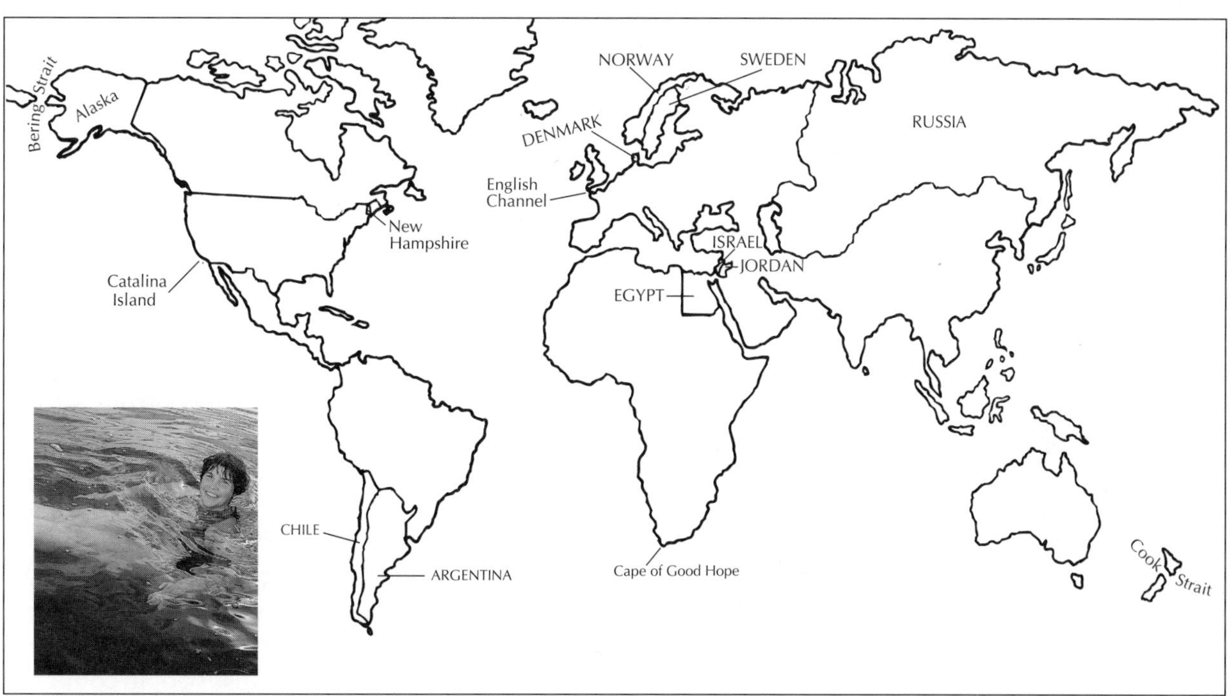

_____ borders	_____ heart	_____ pools	_____ swimsuits
_____ California	_____ hospitals	_____ prizes	_____ teams
_____ cold	_____ oceans	_____ races	
_____ family	_____ Olympics	_____ Russia	
_____ fat	_____ peace	_____ sharks	

Now read the text and check your ideas.

Swimming to Open Up Borders

1 When most people think of swimming, they think of summertime and a hot day at the beach. Lynne Cox thinks of icy cold water, of dolphins, sharks, and jellyfish, and of 20-foot waves. Why? Lynne is an open-water swimmer. Open-water swimmers do not swim in pools but in lakes, seas, and oceans. They swim in some of the most dangerous waters in the world, trying to break records for the fastest time.

2 Lynne was born in 1957 in the state of New Hampshire. She started swimming at the age of 5. Her parents, who were both swimmers, encouraged her love of swimming, especially ocean swimming. Then, when Lynne was 12, the family moved to Southern California. Here Lynne could swim in the ocean year round.

3 In 1971, at the age of 14, Lynne made the 27-mile swim to Catalina, an island off the coast of California. This swim was just the beginning. At age 17, Lynne swam the English Channel, in just 9 hours and 57 minutes. This time of under 10 hours broke the women's record by three hours and the men's record by one hour. Then, in 1975, she swam, beside a group of dolphins, across Cook Strait in New Zealand. In 1977, she swam between Norway and Sweden and between Sweden and Denmark. During these swims, she had to keep away from 3-foot-long jellyfish. The next year, she swam in 20-foot waves around Africa's Cape of Good Hope, watching for sharks all the way. At one point, a 12-foot shark came so close that a helper on a boat had to use a gun to scare it away. Often, Lynne was the first person ever to do these swims. And most of the swims were in very, very cold water, with temperatures as low as 44° F (6.7° C).

4 Lynne's ability to tolerate very cold water is part of the reason that she's such an outstanding open-water swimmer. Most people could not survive for more than about 30 minutes in water that's 44° F, but Lynne can swim in water that cold for hours. In fact, Lynne's body temperature often rises when she swims in cold water. Doctors have found that Lynne has an extra layer of fat around her heart, liver, and other organs. This fat keeps her warm in cold water.

5 People admired Lynne as a great athlete: She broke records, survived cold temperatures and other dangers, and swam where no one ever swam before. But Lynne decided she wanted to use her talent to do something more. She wanted to encourage peace and to help improve relations between countries. In the 1980s, relations between the United

States and Russia were not very good. Lynne decided to swim the 2.7 miles across the Bering Strait, from Alaska, in the United States, to Russia. Lynne wanted the challenge of swimming the extremely cold water (38°–44° F [3.3°–6.7° C]) of the Bering Strait. But even more, Lynne wanted to bring the two countries together. She had to write many letters before the two governments agreed to the swim. Finally, in 1987, she swam across the strait—and both President Mikhail Gorbachev and President Ronald Reagan celebrated her achievement.

6 Lynne continues to make swims that she hopes will help bring countries together. For example, in 1990, she swam between Argentina and Chile. And to support peace in the Middle East, she swam the Gulf of Aqaba from Egypt to Israel and from Israel to Jordan. "By swimming from one national boundary to another," Lynne says, "I hope to push the borders open a little further."

B. READING FOR MAIN IDEAS

Match the sentence beginnings on the left with the sentence endings on the right.

1. Lynne Cox breaks a lot of records _____
2. Lynne Cox can swim in very cold water _____
3. Lynne Cox swims between countries _____

a. because she wants to encourage peace.
b. because she is very fast and can tolerate cold water.
c. because she has an extra layer of fat around her organs.

C. READING FOR DETAILS

1 *Put the sentences in order by time. Write* **1** *next to the sentence that tells what happened first,* **2** *next to the sentence that tells what happened second, and so on.*

_____ Lynne breaks the English Channel record.

_____ Lynne swims off the coast of Southern California.

_____ Lynne swims across the Bering Strait.

_____ Lynne swims between Argentina and Chile.

_____ Lynne swims around the Cape of Good Hope.

2 *Complete the sentences with the number in the list that follows. The first one has been done for you.*

10 30 12 3 2.7 38 ~~5~~

1. Lynne Cox started to swim when she was __5__ years old.
2. She swam _____ miles across the Bering Strait.
3. The water in the Bering Strait was as cold as _____ degrees Fahrenheit.
4. Lynne swam the English Channel in less than _____ hours.
5. When Lynne was swimming around the Cape of Good Hope, a _____-foot shark came too close.
6. When she was swimming near Sweden, she had to watch out for _____-foot-long jellyfish.
7. Most people would die after about _____ minutes in very cold water.

D. READING BETWEEN THE LINES

Read the following statements. Based on the biography, do you agree or disagree? Why? Discuss your answers with the class.

1. Without the extra layer of fat, Lynne Cox would not be a very good open-water swimmer.
2. Very cold water is the greatest danger that Lynne Cox faces.
3. Lynne Cox now swims only to help open borders between countries.
4. Lynne Cox's swims can succeed in improving relations between countries.
5. Lynne Cox's swimming records are not as important as her peace-making efforts.

4

READING TWO: The Athlete's Life

A. EXPANDING THE TOPIC

A vita is a list of the most important events in a person's life with the dates of these events. Read the following vitae of three athletes.

Vita of Edson Arantes do Nascimento "Pele"	
1940	Born in Tres Coracoes, Brazil
1945	Started to play soccer in the streets
1956	Started to play professionally for the Brazilian team Santos
1958	Scored two goals in World Cup final, which Brazil won
1962	Helped Brazil win World Cup
1969	Scored his one-thousandth goal
1970	Scored goal in World Cup final, which Brazil won (only person to win three World Cups as player)
1974	Retired from Santos
1975	Joined New York team Cosmos, helping to make soccer popular in United States
1977	Retired from soccer, with an amazing 1,280 goals in 1,362 professional games
1977–Present	Works for UNICEF (United Nations Children's Fund) and other children's causes; travels the world to encourage soccer
1978	Received International Peace Award for his work with children
1980	Named Athlete of the Century

Vita of Grete Waitz

1953	Born in Oslo, Norway
1971	Won Norway's national 800 m and 1,500 m races
1975–76	Set world records for 3,000 m
1978	Won New York City Marathon[1] with a record time of 2:32:30
1978-81	Was world cross-country champion[2]
1979	Became first woman to break 2:30 in a marathon
1983	Was world marathon champion
1984	Won Olympic silver medal in marathon
1984	Started the 5-K Grete Waitz Run for women in Norway; special attention is paid to women from prisons, sick women, and women from poor countries
1988	Won the New York City Marathon for the ninth time
1990	Retired from competition, with 13 wins in the 19 marathons she ran
1990–Present	Holds Grete Waitz Run each year (with over 45,000 runners, the largest women's race in the world); gives speeches encouraging people to stay healthy through sports; has program to help women who are in prison, poor or sick.

Vita of George Foreman

1949	Born in Marshall, Texas
1965	Left high school without finishing; entered Job Corp, a job-training program for teenagers
1966	Started boxing in neighborhood matches
1967	Boxed in his first official fight
1968	Won gold medal Mexico City Olympics; became professional boxer
1969–73	Beat 36 boxers in just 36 months
1973	Beat champion Joe Frazier to become heavyweight champion of the world
1974	Lost world championship to Muhammad Ali
1978	Left boxing; built a church and became its minister
1980	Opened the George Foreman Youth Community Development Center to help teenagers stay out of trouble.
1987	Started boxing again, at age 39
1988–91	Beat 24 boxers to become the number one heavyweight challenger
1991	Fought the much younger Evander Holyfield for the heavyweight championship in a fight called "The Battle of the Ages." Lost the fight in a close decision.
Present	Has record of 69 wins and 3 losses; helps people through youth center and other programs

[1] *marathon:* a 26-mile 385 yards (42.2k) race
[2] *cross-country:* distance race across land, instead of on roads

B. LINKING READINGS ONE AND TWO

1 *Look at the vita on pages 87–88 and the biography of Lynne Cox. Write down important events in Lynne's life in the form of a vita.*

DATE	EVENT
________	____
________	____
________	____
________	____
________	____
________	____
________	____
________	____
________	____

2 *In a group of three or four, look at and discuss the lives of the four athletes. All of these athletes are people that we can admire. Decide which athlete you admire* ***the most*** *and which you admire* ***the least.*** *For each athlete, think about the following things:*

- What challenges did he or she face, in sports and in life?
- How talented is he or she?
- How hardworking was he or she?
- How great were his or her athletic achievements?
- What did he or she achieve outside sports—in other areas of life?

We admire _______________ the most.

We admire _______________ the least.

Discuss your decisions with the class.

5

REVIEWING LANGUAGE

A. EXPLORING LANGUAGE

Work with a partner. Match each situation on the left with the ***most appropriate*** *quote from the coach, on the right. The first one has been done for you.*

__b__ 1. Encouraging a player to accept a challenge.

____ 2. Telling a player that he is outstanding.

____ 3. Telling a player to tolerate a difficulty.

____ 4. Complimenting a player who broke a record.

____ 5. Summarizing the team's achievement.

____ 6. Praising a player for her talent.

a. "Put up with it just a little longer."

b. "It's hard. But I know you can do it."

c. "You ran that race faster than anyone ever ran it before."

d. "You did very well this year: Twelve wins and only two losses."

e. "You're better than most players I know of. You're the best player on the team."

f. "You're a natural athlete."

B. WORKING WITH WORDS

Complete the crossword clues with words from the following list. Then fill in the crossword puzzle.

borders	encouraged	organs	tolerate
broke	national	outstanding	waves

ACROSS

3. Athletes' hearts, lungs, and other major ________ are in excellent condition.
4. An open-water swimmer must ________ cold.
5. In the water, Lynne Cox can't see the ________ she crosses.
6. First, she ran in small local races; then when she was good enough, she ran in ________ races.

DOWN

1. Big ________ are a problem—they make swimming difficult.
2. She lost the race and wanted to quit, but her friends ________ her to try again.
3. He was a(n) ________ boxer; he won the heavyweight championship.
5. In 1992, Yoko ________ the world record for speed skating 1,000 meters.

6 SKILLS FOR EXPRESSION

A. GRAMMAR: Present Progressive: Affirmative and Negative Statements

1 *Two TV reporters are covering Lynne Cox's swim across the Bering Strait. Read their conversation and notice the underlined words. Then answer the questions that follow.*

NEWSPERSON 1: Welcome to "Today's Sports." As you can see, I'm standing here on a boat just off the Alaskan coast, with my partner, Jim Smith. Today we're joining Lynne Cox, the world-famous open-water swimmer.

NEWSPERSON 2: That's right. Lynne holds the world record for the longest swim in cold water. Today she's planning to swim from Alaska to Russia, a distance of 2.7 miles, in water that's about 40 degrees Fahrenheit.

NEWSPERSON 1: I don't know how she can do it. I'm wearing a heavy jacket and I'm freezing. And Lynne's going into the water, and she isn't wearing anything but a bathing suit!

NEWSPERSON 2: Right now, she's getting ready to go in the water from her boat. The boat will go with her across the strait, so the crew members are preparing to follow her.

NEWSPERSON 1: Now she's in and she's swimming!

NEWSPERSON 2: This has got to be exciting for her. She planned this swim for two years, and now, finally, she's doing it.

1. What part of speech are the underlined words? ____________
2. What do you notice about the endings on the words? ____________
3. Are the people talking about actions that happen often or actions that are happening now?____________

FOCUS ON GRAMMAR

See Present Progressive Statements in *Focus on Grammar, Basic*. See Appendix 13 of *Focus on Grammar, Basic* for more on spelling rules for adding *-ing* to the base form of verbs.

The Present Progressive Tense

Use the **present progressive** (sometimes called present continuous) to talk about an action that is happening right now (at the time you are speaking).

Right now, the swimmers **are jumping** in the water.

To form the present progressive in affirmative statements, use *be* + the base form of the verb.

Subject	*Be*	Base Form + *-ing*
I	**am**	
You	**are**	
He/She/It	**is**	**working**
We/You/They	**are**	

To form the present progressive in negative statements, add *not* after the verb *be*.

Subject	*Be*	*Not*	Base Form + *-ing*
I	**am**		
You	**are**		
He/She/It	**is**	**not**	**working**
We/You/They	**are**		

Use contractions when using the present progressive in speech or informal writing.

I'm learning to speed skate.

She **isn't swimming.**

When adding *-ing* to the base form, remember:

- when a verb ends in a silent *e*, drop the *e* before adding *-ing*

  skate → skat**ing**

- when a one-syllable verb ends in a consonant, a vowel, and a consonant (CVC), double the last consonant before adding *-ing*

  run → run**ning**

Exception: the last consonant is *w*, *x*, or *y*

play → play**ing**

2 *Use the words to write sentences. The first one has been done for you.*

1. at / I / my / friend / smiling / am

   I'm smiling at my friend.

2. biking / is / across / Robin / America / not

   ____

3. soccer / They / playing / in / not / park / are / the

   ____

4. to / game / We / trying / win / are / this

   ____

3 *Complete the paragraph using the present progressive tense of the verbs provided. Use contractions. The first two have been done for you.*

I 'm watching (1. watch) a football game. My team 's playing (2. play) for the championship. For once I ________ (3. not/watch) the game on TV. I was finally able to get a ticket, and I'm actually at the stadium! My team's quarterback ________ (4. throw) the ball to one of his receivers. The receiver ________ (5. run) down the field. The players on the other team ________ (6. try) to stop the receiver from catching the ball. But I think they ________ (7. not/run) fast enough. I think he might be able to catch the ball! But the man in front of me ________ (8. jump) up and down. He ________ (9. make) it impossible for me to see what ________ (10. happen). Too bad I ________ (11. not/sit) at home in front of my TV!

❹ *Use the present progressive tense to describe what is happening in the picture. Write affirmative and negative statements. You can use the verbs from the list. Use contractions.*

clap
fall down
fly
give
help
run
shine
smile
win

Example: Three people are running a race. The woman is winning. The other two aren't winning.

____

____

____

____

B. STYLE: Transition Words of Time

❶ *Read the following two paragraphs. Each paragraph tells the history of Lynne Cox's cold-water swims. Then discuss the questions that follow.*

Lynne Cox is a very experienced cold-water swimmer. She swam in the cold waters of the Atlantic when she was five and her family lived in New Hampshire. She swam year round in the cold waters of the Pacific after her family moved to California when she was twelve. She swam the English Channel, New Zealand's Cook Strait, and many other bodies of water—most of them very cold. She swam the Bering Strait—at only 38° F, this was the coldest water of all.

Lynne Cox is a very experienced cold-water swimmer. First, she swam in the cold waters of the Atlantic when she was five and her family lived in New Hampshire. Then, she swam year round in the cold waters of the Pacific after her family moved to California when she was twelve. Next, she swam the English Channel, New Zealand's Cook Strait, and many other bodies of water—most of them very cold. Finally, she swam the Bering Strait—at only 38° F, this was the coldest water of all.

Which one of the two paragraphs sounds better and is easier to understand? Why?

Transition Words of Time

Transition words are used to show the relationships between the sentences in a piece of writing. **Transition words of time** are used to show time relationships. They help the reader understand which event happened first, which happened second, and so on.

Transition words of time include *first, then, next,* and *later,* which have similar meanings, and *finally.*

Notice that a transition word at the beginning of a sentence is followed by a comma.

- **Then**, she swam in the cold waters of the Pacific Ocean.

2 *Read the story of speed skater Bonnie Blair. Complete the story with transition words of time from the following list. You may use some more than once.*

finally first next then

Bonnie Blair could skate by the time she was two years old, and by the age of four, she was in races. (1) ______________, she skated in group races. (2) ______________, she took up speed skating, where only two skaters race at a time. She won many races. (3) ______________, in 1984, she made the U.S. Olympic team, but she didn't win any medals. (4) ______________, in 1988, Bonnie Blair made the U.S. Olympic team again, and this time she won both gold and bronze medals.

3 *Write a paragraph about runner Kip Keino from Kenya. Use the sentences on the next page in the order they are given and the appropriate transition words of time. (Put a transition word in front of some sentences, but not every one. This would make your sentences sound too much alike.)*

Kip Keino was born in Kenya in 1940.
He has a long history as an outstanding athlete.
Kip Keino started running when he was in elementary school.
He studied at a school for police and ran while he was there.
He raced in national races.
In 1962, he began to race internationally.
He went to the Tokyo Olympics, in 1964, but won nothing.
He went to the Mexico City Olympics four years later and won a gold medal in the 1,500-meter race.
At the Munich Olympics, in 1972, he won a gold medal in the 3,000-meter steeplechase.

____

____

____

____

____

____

____

____

____

4 *Use the information about one of the athletes in Section 4A, pages 87–88, to write a short biography. Use the appropriate transition words of time.*

7 ON YOUR OWN

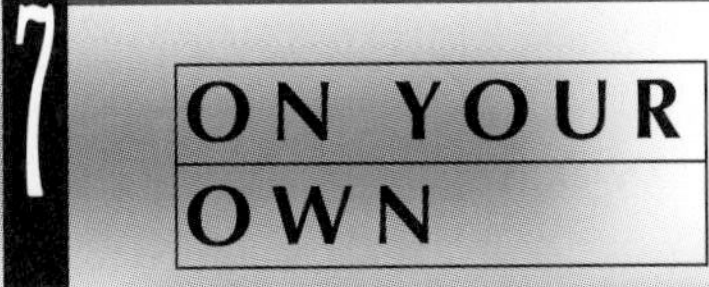

A. WRITING TOPICS

Choose one of the following topics. Write one or two paragraphs. Use some of the vocabulary, grammar, and style that you learned in this unit.

1. Find an old photo or draw a picture of yourself doing a sports activity. Using the present progressive tense, describe the picture. Alternatives: Find a sports picture you like and describe it. Or, draw a picture of your favorite team in action and describe what is happening in the picture.

2. Lynne Cox is often called the "swimming ambassador." Explain why she is called this. (An ambassador is a government employee from one country who works in another country to help build understanding and friendship between the two countries.)

3. Look again at the story of Lynne Cox and at the vitae of the athletes in Section 4A, pages 87–88. What do you think it takes to be a great athelete? You can use Lynne Cox and the other athletes as examples in your paragraphs.

B. FIELDWORK

Write your own biography of an athlete. Follow these steps:

1. Contact an athlete at your school or in your community. (The athlete can be a professional athlete who makes money doing a sport. The athlete can also be your friend who goes running twice a week.)

2. In an interview, ask your athlete the following questions:

   Where and when were you born?

   What sport do you do?

   How old were you when you started to ____________?

   What races or awards have you won, and when were they?

   What other special events have happened in your life? When?

   Other questions:

   ____

   ____

   ____

3. Write a short vita for this athlete.

4. Write a short biography of the athlete. Use appropriate transition words of time.

UNIT 6

SCRUB, SCOUR, AND SMILE!

"ME FIRST! This is the day I put Drāno in all the drains!"

Dangerous sewer germs lurk in every drain. No liquid disinfectant can budge the muck they breed in. It takes Drāno to unclog drains and keep them running free and clear. Use Drāno once a week—every week. Won't harm septic tanks. Makes them work better. Get Drāno today at your grocery or hardware store. Also available in Canada.

Drāno ®

"OK" for all Septic tank systems
She knows—scientific tests proved it to her—that Sani-Flush can't harm any septic tank system. So she happily uses Sani-Flush to clean the toilet bowl—no messy scrubbing. Sani-Flush cleans and disinfects, removes invisible film where germs lurk. Quick, easy, sanitary. Follow directions on can.
Would you like to see the proof? Write for "Report of Scientific Tests." The Hygienic Products Company, Dept. 29, Canton 2, Ohio.

Sani-Flush
Sani-Flush
Guaranteed by Good Housekeeping

No WASH, No WIPE TONIGHT!
New DREFT does both and dishes SHINE
No Wash- No Wipe, Tonight! No Wash- No Wipe, Tonight!
Self-Washing Dreft Means No Work Left No Wash, No Wipe Tonight
...... All YOU do is RINSE! Even pots and pans glisten!
You don't wash... Instead of washing dishes just let them soak in warm Dreft suds for 2 minutes. Dreft floats grease and food particles away. Your hands barely touch the dishwater. All you have to do is rinse the dishes, giving a swish of the cloth where needed, and presto! They're done!
You don't wipe... New Self-Washing Dreft leaves no dishwater film. It washes dishes and glasses so clean, they shine—even without wiping.
You don't scour... Even pots and pans practically soak clean. Dreft's amazing "float-away" action gets under grease—lifts it off—rinses it away—without hard scouring.
It's magic... sheer magic ...it's self-washing!
BEAUTY TIP!
New Dreft is so mild, and your hands are in water so little, it leaves hands beautifully white and soft!
dreft

Advertisements from *Today's Woman*, September 1951, pp. 26, 171, 174.

1 APPROACHING THE TOPIC

A. PREDICTING

Look at the advertisements from a magazine for women, from the 1950s. Discuss your answers to these questions.

1. **What is each advertisement selling?**
2. **Who are the people in the ads?**
3. **What are they doing?**
4. **How do you think they feel?**
5. **Do you smile when you do housework?**

B. SHARING INFORMATION

Who usually does the following chores in the home you live in now? Who usually did the chores in your home when you were growing up? Circle your answers. Then compare answers with a classmate.

	IN YOUR HOME NOW					IN YOUR HOME WHEN YOU WERE GROWING UP				
	Always Men	**Usually Men**	**Sometimes Men, Sometimes Women**	**Usually Women**	**Always Women**	**Always Men**	**Usually Men**	**Sometimes Men, Sometimes Women**	**Usually Women**	**Always Women**
1. Who takes/took care of children?	A	B	C	D	E	A	B	C	D	E
2. Who washes/ washed the dishes?	A	B	C	D	E	A	B	C	D	E
3. Who takes/took out the garbage?	A	B	C	D	E	A	B	C	D	E
4. Who cooks/ cooked?	A	B	C	D	E	A	B	C	D	E
5. Who does/did the laundry?	A	B	C	D	E	A	B	C	D	E

2 PREPARING TO READ

A. BACKGROUND

Look at the chart. Read the sentences that follow the chart. Decide if the sentences are true or false. Write **T** *or* **F** *next to each sentence.*

HOURS PER WEEK SPENT ON HOUSEWORK FOR AMERICAN WOMEN AND MEN

Year	Women	Men
1950s	30–35	6
1990s	20-25	7

_____ **1.** In the 1950s women did more housework than they did in the 1990s.

_____ **2.** In the 1990s men did less housework than in the 1950s.

_____ **3.** In the 1990s women and men did the same amount of housework.

_____ **4.** In the 1950s women did more housework than men.

B. VOCABULARY FOR COMPREHENSION

What do we use these cleaning products and tools for? Draw a line from each cleaning product or tool to the phrase that tells what it is used for.

to clean the windows	to polish a silver cup	to wash dishes
to dust the furniture	to scrub a pot or skillet	to wax the furniture
to make clothes whiter	to scrub the tub or sink	to wipe the table
to mop the floor	to wash clothes	

3

READING ONE: Housework

A. INTRODUCING THE TOPIC

Look at the title of the following poem and read the first stanza (the first section). Circle the types of housework that you think the poem will mention. You may also add more types of housework to the list.

mowing the lawn	washing clothes	vacuuming the rugs
mopping the floors	washing the dishes	putting clothes away

_______________ _______________

_______________ _______________

Read the whole poem and see if the items you chose are correct.

Housework
by Sheldon Harnick

1 *You know, there are times when we happen to be*
just sitting there quietly watching TV,
when the program we're watching will stop for awhile
and suddenly someone appears with a smile
and starts to show us how terribly urgent it is to buy some brand of detergent
or soap or cleanser or cleaner or powder or paste or wax or bleach—
to help with the housework.

2 *Now, most of the time it's a lady we see who's doing the housework on the TV.*
She's cheerfully scouring[1] *a skillet or two,*
or she's polishing pots 'til they gleam[2] *like new,*
or she's scrubbing the tub, or she's mopping the floors,
or she's wiping the stains from the walls and the doors,
or she's washing the windows, the dishes, the clothes,
or waxing the furniture 'til it just glows,
or cleaning the "fridge,"[3] *or the stove or the sink*
with a lighthearted[4] *smile and a friendly wink*
and she's doing her best to make us think that her *soap*
(or detergent or cleanser or cleaner or powder or paste or wax or bleach)
is the best kind of soap
(or detergent or cleanser or cleaner or powder or paste or wax or bleach)
that there is in the whole wide world!

---

[1] *to scour:* to scrub
[2] *to gleam:* to shine
[3] *fridge:* refrigerator
[4] *lighthearted:* cheerful

3 19 *And maybe it is. . .*
20 *and maybe it isn't. . .*
21 *and maybe it does what they say it will do. . .*
22 *but I'll tell you one thing I know is true:*
23 *The lady we see when we're watching TV—*
24 *The lady who smiles as she scours*
or scrubs or rubs or washes or wipes or mops or dusts or cleans—
25 *or whatever she does on our TV screens—*
26 *that lady is smiling because she's an actress.*
27 *And she's earning money for learning those speeches that mention those wonderful soaps and detergents and cleansers and cleaners and powders and pastes and waxes and bleaches.*

4 28 *So the very next time that you happen to be*
29 *just sitting there quietly watching TV,*
30 *and you see some nice lady who smiles as she scours or scrubs or rubs or washes or wipes or mops or dusts or cleans*

5 31 *remember:*
32 *Nobody smiles doing housework but those ladies you see on TV.*
33 *Because even if the soap or detergent or cleanser or cleaner or powder or paste or wax or bleach—*
34 *that you use is the very best one—*
35 *housework is just no fun.*

6 36 *Children,*
37 *when you have a house of your own,*
38 *make sure when there's housework to do that you don't have to do it alone.*
39 *Little boys, little girls,*
40 *when you're big husbands and wives,*
41 *if you want all of the days of your lives to seem sunny as summer weather,*
42 *make sure when there's housework to do that you do it together.*

C. Hart, L. C. Pogrebin, and M. Thomas, eds., *Free to Be You and Me* (New York: McGraw-Hill, 1974).

B. READING FOR MAIN IDEAS

Check (√) the two main ideas in the poem.

____ 1. TV ads give us good information about which soaps and detergents are best.

____ 2. Men and women should share the housework.

____ 3. Children shouldn't watch TV because there are too many ads.

____ 4. Housework isn't really too much fun.

C. READING FOR DETAILS

Read the following sentences. Then for each sentence, look in the stanza mentioned. Find the line or lines that have the same meaning as the sentence. Fill in the line number or numbers. The first one has been done for you.

1. This person tells us that it's important to buy the right brand of cleaning products.

   First stanza, line 5

2. Usually, women do all of the housework on TV.

   Second stanza, line ____

3. She is trying to make us believe that her cleaning product is the best.

   Second stanza, lines ____, ____ *and* ____

4. The TV lady's detergent might really be an excellent detergent.

   Third stanza, lines ____, ____, *and* ____

5. The lady on TV looks happy because it is her job.

   Third stanza, line ____

6. Only actresses on TV ads smile while they do housework. Other people never smile when they do housework.

   Fifth stanza, line ____

7. Good cleaning products don't make housework fun.

   Fifth stanza, lines ____, ____, *and* ____

D. READING BETWEEN THE LINES

Read each statement. Decide if the statement is 1—something that the TV advertisers want us to think, 2—something that the poet wants us to think, and/or 3—your own opinion. Put the letter of the statement in the list(s) where it belongs. The first one has been done for you.

When you finish, compare your answers with those of a partner.

a. Housework is fun if you have the best detergent.

b. Housework is never fun.

c. Most women like doing housework.

d. Some soaps and detergents are better than others.

e. Men should do housework, too.

f. Husbands and wives should share housework if they want to be happy.

g. It's important to do housework.

h. The ladies on TV are the only people who smile while they do the housework.

1. THE TV ADVERTISERS WANT US TO THINK:	2. THE POET WANTS US TO THINK:	3. MY OPINION IS:
a		

READING TWO: Good-bye to (Some) Housework

A. EXPANDING THE TOPIC

Read the following article. Then answer the questions about the article. Check your answers with a partner.

Good-bye to (Some) Housework

1 I can remember a certain TV ad from when I was a child. In this ad, a happy housewife is polishing her table. The table is so shiny that we can see her smiling reflection in it. She's so happy about her shiny table top! Does shiny furniture make people happy anymore? Does anyone even polish furniture anymore? I cannot remember the last time that I polished furniture.

2 People have less time for housework these days. They are lucky if they have time to wipe the crumbs off the table and put the breakfast dishes in the sink before they go to their jobs.

3 Because people have less time, many kinds of chores,[1] like polishing furniture, just don't get done anymore. Some people have studied changes in the use of cleaning products. From their studies, we can tell which chores aren't getting done. For example, one study looked at differences in the types of housework people did between 1986 and 1996. In just ten years, there were many changes.

4 Some chores, like laundry, will never go away. In 1996, people used about the same amount of laundry detergent that they used in 1986. But polishing furniture seems to be less important than doing laundry. In 1986, 21 percent of homemakers[2] used three or more cans of furniture polish in six months. By 1996, only 12 percent of homemakers used that much furniture polish. Carpet cleaning is another endangered chore. In 1986, 9 percent of homemakers used three or more containers of carpet cleaner in six months. By 1996, only 5 percent of homemakers used that much carpet cleaner. And what about those ovens? Seventy-five percent of homemakers used no oven cleaner for six months in 1996!

1. Why are people doing less housework now?
2. Which chore(s) are people doing less often now?
3. Which chore(s) do people do as often today?

Statistics from Mediamark Research, Inc. of New York, cited in *American Demographics*, January, 1997.

[1] *chores:* types of housework

[2] *homemaker:* person in family who is in charge of housework

B. LINKING READINGS ONE AND TWO

The poem in Reading One mentions many types of housework. List these chores in the left column of the chart. Use information from Reading Two to answer the question in the right column. Sometimes the answer will not be clear from the reading, so you will need to make your best guess. Write **as much** *or* **less**. *The first one has been done for you. When you have finished, discuss the questions that follow.*

Chores from "Housework"	Do people today do this chore as much as before or less than before?
scouring skillets	less

1. Why did you give the answers you did to the question on the right?
2. Compare yesterday's and today's chores. How are they different?
3. Do you think that people will continue to do less and less housework in the future? Why or why not? Which other chores do you think might disappear?

5 REVIEWING LANGUAGE

A. EXPLORING LANGUAGE

Cross out the sentence that does not make sense. The first one has been done for you.

1. **a.** I happened to be at the supermarket yesterday when they were giving away free boxes of a new detergent!

   b. Excuse me, do you happen to have change for a dollar?

   c. ~~OK, I'll meet you for lunch tomorrow. I will happen to be there at 12:15.~~

2. **a.** I have a terribly urgent message for Tom. Can you make sure that he gets it this month?

   b. This letter is terribly urgent. I think I should send it express mail, so it gets there tomorrow.

   c. I'd like to talk to Dr. Donlon, but it's not terribly urgent. She can call me back when she has time.

3. **a.** This detergent doesn't make my clothes really clean. Perhaps I should try a different brand.

   b. Bleach is the best brand to use for washing white clothes.

   c. Can you buy some detergent for me? Just get the cheapest brand.

4. **a.** The president winked at the end of his speech about the recent war.

   b. My grandpa used to wink when he told a joke.

   c. Jim winked at the little girl as he said good-bye to her.

5. **a.** Before the Madonna concert, a man came on stage and mentioned, "Here's Madonna!"

   b. Did you mention the party to Joe? I haven't invited him yet.

   c. Please don't mention anything about my vacation plans to my boss. She doesn't think anyone should take vacations.

6. **a.** Diana was surprised when the dinner guests appeared an hour early.

   b. My keys have appeared. I can't find them.

   c. Every time I cook fish for dinner, Tuca, the neighbor's cat, appears at my back door.

7. a. I have a speech with my mom on the telephone every Sunday.
   b. The president gave a speech last night about taxes and education.
   c. I always get nervous when I have to make speeches in my English class.

8. a. Karen wants to be an actress, so she has moved to Hollywood.
   b. A new movie with my favorite actress is opening tonight at the Lumiere theater. Do you want to go?
   c. You need to be really good at math and geometry if you want to be an actor or an actress.

B. WORKING WITH WORDS

Complete the sentences with the following words. Use a word from A for the first blank in each item. Use a word from B for the second blank. The first one has been done for you.

A		B	
actress	happen to	bleach	mop
detergent	mention	cleanser	terribly urgent
glow	polish	dust	winked

1. I don't have time to ___polish___ the furniture, so I am just going to ___dust___ it.
2. ____________ makes clothes clean, but ____________ makes them white.
3. Can you get some dish soap the next time you ____________ be at the store? It's not ____________, so don't make a special trip.
4. If you want your floors to ____________, use new, improved Twinkle-Floor next time you ____________!
5. The woman in the ad didn't ____________ the price of the ____________ that she was using to clean the tub.
6. The ____________ accepted her award and said, "I couldn't have done it without my husband and daughter," as she ____________ at them in the audience.

6 SKILLS FOR EXPRESSION

A. GRAMMAR: Adverbs and Expressions of Frequency

1 *Read the following letter and underline the words and phrases that tell us* ***how often*** *someone does something. Then answer the questions.*

September 5

Dear Mom and Dad,

My second year here is off to a great start. My classes are good, and I have finally found a place to live! It feels like home already. The two guys who live here are just like me when it comes to cleaning! They clean the bathroom about once a month and they never vacuum because they don't have a vacuum cleaner! About once a week, they get together and do all of the dishes. (They wait until there aren't any clean ones left!) I know I will get along with these guys better than with the clean freak I lived with last year.

Do you remember Felix? I talked to him yesterday. He still dusts, sweeps, and mops almost every day! He is so busy with housework that he rarely has time to have fun. I am usually out with friends in the evenings and on weekends. I think he is jealous.

Are you still coming to visit next month? I know that you are both busy. How often do you have to fly to Seattle with this new job, Mom? It sounds like you are there every week.

Anyway, I hope you can come soon. I look forward to seeing you!

Love,
Oscar

1. What are the words and phrases you underlined? ____________________

2. Which verb tense does the writer use in sentences with these words and phrases? ____________________

Focus on Grammar

See Adverbs and Expressions of Frequency in *Focus on Grammar, Basic*.

Adverbs and Expressions of Frequency	
1. Use the simple present tense with an **adverb** or **expression of frequency** to describe how often someone does something.	They **never *vacuum*** because they don't have a vacuum cleaner. I ***am* usually** out with friends in the evenings and on weekends. They ***clean*** the bathroom **about once a month.** **About once a week**, they ***get*** together and ***do*** all of the dishes.
2. Adverbs of frequency (e.g., *always, usually, often, sometimes, rarely, never*) usually go after the verb *be*. But they usually go before other verbs.	I ***am* usually** out with friends in the evenings and on weekends. They **never *vacuum*** because they don't have a vacuum cleaner.
3. Expressions of frequency (e.g., *about once a month, twice a month, once a week, every day*) usually go at the beginning or at the end of sentences.	They clean the bathroom **about once a month**. **About once a week**, they get together and do all of the dishes.
4. Use *How often. . . ?* in questions about frequency.	**How often** do you have to fly to Seattle with this new job, Mom?

2 *Felix is looking for another roommate. He went to a roommate agency and filled out a questionnaire. Use the information in this questionnaire to complete the exercise.*

✣ ROOMMATES FOR YOU ✣

To help us find you the best roommate, please answer the following questions:

Name: Felix M. Jefferson, Jr.

Describe yourself. How often . . .

	Never	Rarely	Sometimes	Usually	Always
. . . do you smoke in the house?	✔				
. . . do you watch TV in the evenings?		✔			
. . . do you have dinner guests?	✔				
. . . do you listen to the radio or CDs?		✔			
. . . are you at home on the weekends?				✔	
. . . do you go to sleep before 11P.M.?					✔

Housekeeping

Answer the following questions with the frequency of each activity (e.g., 1X/week = once a week, 2X/month = twice a month).
How often do you . . .

. . . vacuum the carpets? 2X/week

. . . dust the furniture? 1X/week

. . . mop the floors? every day

. . . clean the bathroom? 3X/week

. . . wash the windows? every week

. . . clean the oven? 2X/month

Add adverbs and expressions of frequency to the following sentences about Felix. The first one has been done for you.

1. Felix smokes in the house.

   Felix never smokes in the house.

2. He listens to the radio or CDs.

   ____

3. He has dinner guests.

   ____

4. He is in bed by 11 P.M.

____

5. He is at home on the weekends.

____

6. He vacuums the carpets.

____

7. He cleans the bathroom.

____

8. He washes the windows.

____

9. He cleans the oven.

____

3 *Write questions with* ***How often... you...*** *about the following chores. Then exchange questions with a partner and let your partner write answers to your questions. The first one has been done for you.*

1. (mop the floors)

   How often do you mop the floors?

   I mop the floors about twice a month.

2. (wash the dishes)

   How often ________________________________

   ____

3. (clean the bathroom)

   How often ________________________________

   ____

4. (dust the furniture)

   How often ________________________________

   ____

5. (stay up late)

   How often ________________________________

   ____

6. (invite people to your home)

   How often ________________________________

   ____

7. (do laundry)
   How often ____

   ____

4 *Look at the answers you gave to your partner in exercise 3. Who would you prefer to live with, Oscar or Felix? Write a short paragraph. Give your reasons for your choice.*

I would prefer to live with ____________ because ____________

____

____

____

____

B. STYLE: Poetry

1 *Read the first stanza of the poem in Reading One out loud several times to yourself. Then read the first paragraph of the text in Reading Two out loud several times. Why does the poem sound different?*

Writing Rhymes

Poems often use words that rhyme with each other. Usually, the words that rhyme are at the end of different lines, but sometimes they are in the same line. Two words **rhyme** if their endings sound the same.

*There once was a big purple **ball**,*
*Which was for a **ball** very **tall**,*
*A boy took a **pin**,*
*And stuck it right **in**,*
*And then there was no **ball** at **all**!*

❷ *Look at the first stanza of "Housework." Find the words that rhyme. Circle the words and connect them with lines. The first ones have been done for you.*

"You know, there are times when we happen to (be,)
just sitting there quietly watching (TV,)
when the program we're watching will stop for awhile,
and suddenly someone appears with a smile,
and starts to show us how terribly urgent it is to buy some brand of
detergent or soap or cleanser or cleaner or powder or paste or wax
or bleach—
to help with the housework."

❸ *Put the following words into lists of words that rhyme. Then add some more words that you know to each list. One word has been done for you.*

awhile	doors	keep	mile	pop
cheap	drop	leap	none	run
~~chores~~	hop	means	pile	shop
done	jeans			

FLOORS	CLEANS	FUN	SMILE	MOP	SWEEP
chores					

❹ *Write two lines about housework and end the lines with words that rhyme.*

Examples: I don't like mopping floors.
It's the worst of all the chores!

I never clean my sinks.
That's why my house stinks!

____

____

____

____

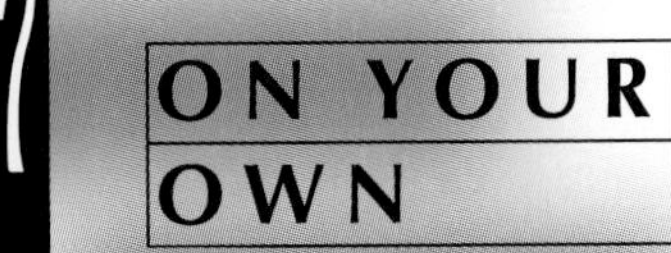

7 ON YOUR OWN

A. WRITING TOPICS

Choose one of the following topics. Write one or two paragraphs. Use some of the vocabulary, grammar, and style that you learned in this unit.

1. Write a poem about housework. Use some rhyming words.

2. Who does the housework in your house? Write about different chores. Who usually does these chores? Who sometimes does them? Who never does them? Does everyone share in the housework? Do some people do more housework than other people?

3. Find an ad with a person in it for a cleaning product on TV or in a magazine. Does the ad have a smiling lady, like the one in the poem? Describe this person. What is the person doing? Does the person look happy?

4. Find an ad for a cleaning product. Describe the ad. According to the ad, why should people buy the product? Who do you think the advertisers are trying to sell the product to—mainly to women who work, mainly to women who stay at home, to all women, to both women and men?

B. FIELDWORK

Work in groups. Write a questionnaire to find out more about what people in your community think about housework.

1. Write five questions, and make a questionnaire. (See the following example.) You will need to make copies to give to the people that you survey.

2. In your groups, decide where each person will hand out the questionnaire. One person might go to a shopping center, and one person might go to a bus stop, for example.

   You also need to decide who you will survey. For example, how many men and how many women will you survey? Do you want to survey people of different ages? Do you want to survey people who live alone *and* people who have families?

3. Each person should survey at least five people. When you have all of your answers, you need to count the answers for each question.

4. Report back to the class about what you learned from your survey.

✯ SAMPLE SURVEY ✯

Please take a few minutes to answer the following questions!
Thank you very much!

			Comments
1. Do you clean your oven at least once a year?	❏ **YES**	❏ **NO**	
2. Do you do laundry at least twice a month?	❏ **YES**	❏ **NO**	
3. Do you vacuum at least once a week?	❏ **YES**	❏ **NO**	
4. Do you ever polish the furniture in your home?	❏ **YES**	❏ **NO**	
5. Do you do as much housework as your parents did?	❏ **YES**	❏ **NO**	

UNIT 7

ORGANIC PRODUCE: IS IT WORTH THE PRICE?

1 APPROACHING THE TOPIC

A. PREDICTING

Look at the picture. What differences do you see between the fruit in each bowl? Which bowl would you choose? Why? Discuss your answers with a partner.

B. SHARING INFORMATION

When you shop, how do you choose your fruit? Do you choose it by its smell? Do you choose it by its color? For each kind of fruit, check (√) each box that shows how you choose that fruit.

FRUIT	SMELL	COLOR	SOFTNESS/ HARDNESS	SIZE	PRICE
Apples	☐	☐	☐	☐	☐
Bananas	☐	☐	☐	☐	☐
Oranges	☐	☐	☐	☐	☐
Pears	☐	☐	☐	☐	☐
Melons	☐	☐	☐	☐	☐
Strawberries	☐	☐	☐	☐	☐
Other:	☐	☐	☐	☐	☐

In a small group, share and discuss your answers. For example, if you checked "size" for apples, what size do you look for? Why?

2 PREPARING TO READ

A. BACKGROUND

Look at the drawing of a produce section of a grocery store on page 121. There are many kinds of fruits and vegetables. Some are "organic." Some are nonorganic (not organic). Use the information in the drawing to complete the sentences. The first one has been done for you.

1. Apples cost $1.39/pound.
2. Organic apples cost ___________.
3. Pears cost ___________.

4. Organic pears cost ___________.
5. There are ___________ kinds of lettuce.
6. Red leaf lettuce costs ___________.
7. Green leaf lettuce costs ___________.
8. Organic green leaf lettuce costs ___________.
9. ___________ lettuce is the most expensive lettuce.

Why do you think organic fruits and vegetables are more expensive? Discuss this question with your classmates.

B. VOCABULARY FOR COMPREHENSION

1 *Read the sentences. Try to understand the underlined words without looking them up in a dictionary. Then match the words to the definitions.*

1. Orange juice really is orange. But many sodas are made with <u>artificial</u> colors. These colors come from chemicals.
2. Sometimes bananas are green and hard. To <u>ripen</u> them, put them in a paper bag. In one or two days, they should be yellow and soft.
3. Some fruits, like apples, grow on trees. Some, like blackberries, grow on bushes. And some, like grapes, grow on <u>vines</u>.
4. The <u>old-fashioned</u> way to make ice cream took a lot of time and hard work. But the way we make ice cream today is fast and easy.
5. <u>Fresh</u> fruit tastes much better than fruit from a can.

_____ 1. artificial	a. become ready to eat
_____ 2. ripen	b. not modern or new
_____ 3. vine	c. not canned or frozen
_____ 4. old-fashioned	d. not natural
_____ 5. fresh	e. a plant that grows up and around a stick

2 *Read the sentences. Try to understand the underlined words without looking them up in a dictionary. Then use the underlined words to complete the chart. Some words are the names of the categories. Other words are examples of things that belong in the categories.*

1. You'll find bananas in the produce section of your market.
2. Farmers use pesticides and herbicides to kill insects and weeds.
3. I hate insects! Mosquitoes bite me every time I go outside. And ants get into all the food in my cupboards.
4. Sometimes I have trouble growing vegetables. But I never have trouble growing weeds! They just take over the garden.
5. Cancer kills millions of people every year.
6. These tomatoes don't look very nice. But they taste wonderful.

CHEMICALS	________	PLANTS	SENSES	________	ILLNESSES
1. ________	**1.** apples	**1.** flowers	**1.** feel	**1.** mosquitoes	**1.** the flu
2. ________	**2.** oranges	**2.** vegetables	**2.** smell	**2.** flies	**2.** a cold
	3. broccoli	**3.** trees	**3.** hear	**3.** ants	**3.** AIDS
	4. lettuce	**4.** ________	**4.** see		**4.** ________
			5. ________		

3 READING ONE: Organic Produce versus Nonorganic Produce

A. INTRODUCING THE TOPIC

Read the letter to Mr. Green. This letter asks two questions. How will Mr. Green answer these questions? Write your ideas for each answer in the spaces that follow.

Dear Mr. Green:

1 Lately I see more and more "organic" fruits and vegetables in the supermarkets. I'm confused. Often the organic apples or strawberries aren't as red or as large as the other ones. They sometimes have spots or insect holes. And organic produce can cost three times as much as other produce! So, tell me, what exactly are organic fruits and vegetables? And why are they so expensive?

Confused Shopper
Bakersfield, CA

1. ______________________________
____

2. ______________________________
____

Now read Mr. Green's answer.

ASK MR. GREEN: Organic Produce versus Nonorganic Produce

Dear Confused Shopper,

1 You're right. Sometimes organic produce doesn't look as nice as nonorganic produce, and it generally costs up to 50 percent more. Let me explain why.

2 Since about 1950, farmers have used chemicals to grow their fruits and vegetables. They use pesticides to kill insects that eat their plants. They use herbicides to kill the weeds that kill their plants. These chemicals are a great help to farmers. By using them, farmers can grow more produce on the same amount of land. This means that shoppers can find more produce in the stores.

3 Farmers even use chemicals to artificially ripen fruits and vegetables. Most tomatoes, for example, are picked from the vine while they are still green. They turn red when chemicals are added to the box as it goes to the supermarket. Because produce can be picked early, it can travel long distances to stores. As a result, we can find most kinds of fruits and vegetables all year long.

4 Some people argue, however, that there are problems with using all these chemicals. When we eat produce, we're also eating a little bit of the chemicals. Over time, these chemicals build up in our bodies. Some scientists believe that this build up of chemicals can even cause cancer. Because of worries like these, some farmers now grow produce the old-fashioned way—without chemicals. We call this kind of produce "organic."

5 Organic produce is more expensive than other produce for several reasons. Many organic farmers can't grow as much produce as other farmers. Their farms tend to be smaller, and, of course, they don't use herbicides and pesticides. And because no chemicals are used, the produce has to arrive at the store very soon after it's picked. This, too, costs money.

6 Is organic produce worth the extra cost? Should you buy organic produce or nonorganic produce? That's up to you. But, if you're not familiar with organic produce, you might want to try it. More and more shoppers are buying organic produce. And many of these shoppers say that they're not just concerned about their health. They say organic fruits and vegetables taste fresher and better.

B. READING FOR MAIN IDEAS

Check (√) the ideas that Mr. Green discussed in his letter.

_____ **1.** He explained how much organic fruits and vegetables cost.

_____ **2.** He discussed the first farmers to grow organic produce.

_____ **3.** He discussed the use of chemicals in growing nonorganic produce.

_____ **4.** He explained why nonorganic produce may be bad for your health.

_____ **5.** He explained what organic produce is.

_____ **6.** He explained why organic fruits and vegetables are expensive.

_____ **7.** He explained where people can buy organic produce.

C. READING FOR DETAILS

Decide if the statements are true or false. Write **T** *or* **F** *next to each statement. If the statement is false, write a true statement after it. The first one has been done for you.*

__F__ **1.** Organic produce looks the same as nonorganic produce.

Organic produce doesn't look as nice as nonorganic produce.

_____ **2.** Organic produce generally costs up to 50 percent more than nonorganic produce.

____

_____ **3.** Herbicides kill insects.

____

_____ **4.** Some scientists believe that chemical buildup can cause heart problems.

____

_____ **5.** Organic fruits and vegetables are ripened with chemicals.

____

_____ 6. With chemicals, farmers can grow more produce on the same amount of land.

____

_____ 7. Organic produce has to arrive at stores quickly.

____

D. READING BETWEEN THE LINES

Read each quote. Decide whether the person who said it would probably buy organic or nonorganic produce. Write ***organic*** *or* ***nonorganic****. Then discuss your answers with those of a partner.*

1. "I think that nowadays even the air we breathe is harmful." _____________
2. "I don't want to wait until summer for strawberries." _____________
3. "I like apples that taste like the apples we picked off trees when I was a kid." _____________
4. "I'm trying not to spend much money on food this month." _____________
5. "It might sound silly—but I always want the things that look the nicest." _____________
6. "I don't want to feed my children any foods that might not be healthy for them." _____________

4 READING TWO: What's in Our Food?

A. EXPANDING THE TOPIC

Chemicals aren't just used to grow produce. They are also used to keep foods fresh, give them color, or change the taste. "Natural food," including organic food, is food that doesn't have any chemicals or other artificial ingredients.

Look quickly at the two soup can labels.

Which soup is natural? ________________

Which soup has artificial ingredients? ________________

Read the labels more carefully. Then work in a small group to answer the questions that follow.

WHAT'S IN OUR FOOD?

Label 1: Gordon's Soup

Nutrition Facts

Serving[1] Size ½ cup (120 ml)
Servings Per Container 2.5

Amount Per Serving:

Calories 80 Calories from Fat 20

	% Daily Value[2]
Total Fat 2g	3%
Saturated Fat 1g	5%
Cholesterol 10mg	3%
Sodium 810mg	34%
Total Carbohydrate 10g	3%
Dietary Fiber 2g	8%
Sugars 2g	
Protein 5g	

Vitamin A 40% • Vitamin C 0%
Calcium 2% • Iron 4%

Ingredients: potatoes, carrots, water, green beans, peas, salt, onions, celery, tomato paste, vegetable oil, monosodium glutamate, caramel color, and sugar.

Label 2: Health Country Soup

Nutrition Facts

Serving Size 1 cup (240g)
Servings Per Container 2

Amount Per Serving:

Calories 80 Calories from Fat 0

	% Daily Value
Total Fat 0g	0%
Saturated Fat 0g	0%
Cholesterol 0mg	0%
Sodium 250mg	10%
Total Carbohydrate 17g	6%
Dietary Fiber 4g	16%
Sugars 8g	
Protein 6g	

Vitamin A 200% • Vitamin C 25%
Calcium 4% • Iron 10%

Ingredients: water, organic carrots, organic tomatoes, organic celery, organic potatoes, organic peas, organic green beans, tomato paste, small white beans, honey, organic lima beans, organic onions, organic broccoli, organic cabbage, organic cauliflower, organic spinach, sea salt, organic green peppers, garlic, lemon juice, pepper, parsley, nutmeg, bay leaves, sage, basil, oregano.

---

[1] *serving:* an amount for one person
[2] *% daily value:* how much the food gives you of what a person needs in a day

1. Which can has more soup? ____________
2. Which soup has more fat per serving? ____________
3. Which soup has more sodium (salt) per serving? ____________
4. Which soup has more protein per serving? ____________
5. Which soup has more vitamins and minerals (calcium, iron) per serving? ____________
6. Which vegetables are in both soups? ________________________

   ____

   ____
7. What vegetables, if any, are in the Health Country soup but not in the Gordon's soup? ________________________

   ____

   ____
8. What vegetables, if any, are in the Gordon's soup but not in the Health Country soup? ________________________

   ____

   ____
9. What difference is there between the vegetables in the Gordon's soup and the vegetables in the Health Country soup? ____________

   ____
10. Spices are natural ingredients added to foods to make them taste better and more interesting. What spices do you recognize on these labels? ________________________

    Which soup has these spices? ________________________
11. What other ingredients do you see on the Gordon's soup label?

    ____

    Why do you think these ingredients are added to the soup?

    ____
12. Which soup do you think is better for you? ____________

    Discuss why.

B. LINKING READINGS ONE AND TWO

You own a small restaurant. Many customers are asking for soup, so you want to add a homemade vegetable soup to your menu. But you have two vegetable soup recipes. One is for a soup that's like Gordon's soup. The other uses lots of organic vegetables, like Health Country's soup. Which recipe should you use?

In a small group, think about and discuss the following things and then make your decision:

- Price: Which soup will cost less for you (and your customers), the natural soup or the other soup?
- Taste: Which soup will customers like better?
- Customer concerns and likes: These days, what worries about food do many people have? What kinds of produce are more and more people buying?
- Availability of produce: Will you be able to find the vegetables you need all year long?
- Time: How long will these soups take to make?

Which recipe will your restaurant use? ____________________

Discuss your decision and the reasons for it with the class.

5 REVIEWING LANGUAGE

A. EXPLORING LANGUAGE

Read the conversation between a radio program interviewer and a farmer. Complete the conversation, using the words that follow. The first one has been done for you.

fresh	natural	produce	~~vines~~
herbicides	old-fashioned	ripen	weeds
insects	pesticides	tastes	

INTERVIEWER: Today I'm talking to Mr. Robinson, who runs an organic farm. We're in a field with many (1) ___vines___ full of tomatoes that are starting to (2) ____________ . Mr. Robinson, can you tell us about this new way of farming?

MR. ROBINSON: Actually, organic farming is not new; it's really the (3) ____________ way of farming. I grow (4) ____________ without using (5) ____________ to kill weeds or (6) ____________ to kill insects.

INTERVIEWER: How do you keep (7) ____________ from eating your plants?

MR. ROBINSON: Well, I do lose some plants to them. But there are many things I can do.

INTERVIEWER: For example . . . ?

MR. ROBINSON: Do you see the little yellow flowers next to the tomatoes? They are marigolds. The insects don't like the smell of the marigolds, so they stay away from the tomatoes. This method is easy and it's (8) ____________ .

INTERVIEWER: What else do you do?

MR. ROBINSON: I make sure I get rid of all the (9) ____________ because they're plants I don't want and harmful insects like them. And then, believe it or not, some insects are good insects. They don't harm plants, and they kill insects that do harm plants. So I make sure there are lots of good insects here.

INTERVIEWER: All this sounds like a lot of work.

MR. ROBINSON: It is hard work, but it's worth it. People want produce that (10) ____________ (11) ____________ . I grow it for them!

B. WORKING WITH WORDS

Cross out the word or phrase that is not related to the boldfaced word. The first one has been done for you.

1. **herbicides:** ~~insects~~, weeds, farms
2. **ripe:** yellow banana, green strawberry, red apple
3. **vines:** tomatoes, plants, apples
4. **pesticides:** insects, weeds, chemicals
5. **artificial:** caramel color, monosodium glutamate, carrot
6. **produce:** potato, apple, soup
7. **taste:** bad, hard, fresh
8. **old-fashioned:** milking cows by hand, separating eggs with an electric machine, planting corn with a stick

6 SKILLS FOR EXPRESSION

A. GRAMMAR: Count and Non-Count Nouns

1 *Read the note and underline all the food words in the second paragraph. The first one has been done for you. Then answer the questions that follow.*

Hi Matt,

I won't be home until 7:30. Can you go to the store? I want to make spaghetti and a salad for dinner, but we don't have everything we need. And we also need some food for the weekend.

For tonight, can you get some <u>spaghetti</u>, some onions, some lettuce, and tomatoes? And how about a watermelon for dessert?

We'll need bread and eggs for breakfast tomorrow. I noticed that we're almost out of rice and milk. I also thought it would be nice to have some more fruit in the house. Could you buy bananas and grapes? Oh, and how about a cake for dessert, too?

If you go to Rainbow Grocery, then buy all organic produce. See you later.

Love,

Alice

1. Which food words in the second paragraph are singular? What word comes before a singular food word?

2. Which food words in the second paragraph are plural? What is the last letter in the plural food words?

FOCUS ON GRAMMAR

See Count and Non-Count Nouns in *Focus on Grammar, Basic.*

Count and Non-Count Nouns

Some nouns can be counted. These are called **count nouns**. Use *a, an,* or *one* before a singular count noun. Plural count nouns need only *-s* or *-es* at the end of the word.	I need **an** onion. I need **a** tomato.	I need onion**s**. I need tomato**es**.
Some nouns can't be counted. These are called **non-count nouns**. They do not have a plural form. Do not use *a, an,* or a number before non-count nouns. Do not add *-s* or *-es* to non-count nouns.	I buy produce at the supermarket. We have bread.	
Some can be used with plural count nouns and non-count nouns in affirmative statements.	I need **some** onions. (count) I need **some** milk. (non-count)	
Use *any* with plural count nouns and non-count nouns in negative statements.	I don't have **any** onions. (count) I don't have **any** milk. (non-count)	
A lot of can be used with plural count nouns and with non-count nouns.	I need **a lot of** onions. (count) I need **a lot of** milk. (non-count)	

2 *Find all the food items in the note in exercise 1 and do the following:*

1. Circle all the singular count nouns.
2. Put a square around all the plural count nouns.
3. Underline all the non-count nouns two times.

Check your answers with classmates.

3 *Complete the paragraph with count nouns and non-count nouns. Make the nouns plural where necessary. The first one has been done for you.*

Matt went to the store. He bought ____eggs____ (1. egg), ________ (2. rice), ________ (3. spaghetti), ________ (4. milk), and ________ (5. bread). But the store didn't have any organic ________ (6. produce). So, he went to the natural grocery store across town. There he bought ________ (7. lettuce), ________ (8. tomato), ________ (9. banana), and ________ (10. grape). But he forgot to buy a ________ (11. watermelon).

4 *Work with a partner. Alice wants to make garden burgers. She has a lot of milk and eggs in her refrigerator. Read the recipe, and look at the food Alice has in her cupboard. Write sentences about what food she has a lot of, what food she doesn't have, and what food she has but needs to buy more of. Use* **some, a lot of,** *and* **any.** *Use* **a** *and* **an** *with singular count nouns. Follow the examples.*

Garden Burgers

Ingredients

3 cups of walnuts
2 cups of rolled oats
4 eggs
$\frac{1}{2}$ cup milk
oil (for frying)
3 cups water
1 onion
1 green pepper
1 carrot
1 teaspoon salt
$\frac{1}{4}$ teaspoon pepper

Directions

Chop walnuts and vegetables. Mix the chopped walnuts and vegetables with oats, eggs, milk, salt, and pepper. Make small balls, about 3 inches across. Make the balls flat with the back of a spoon and fry in oil until brown. Add water to pan and cook patties in boiling water for 25 minutes.

1. She has a lot of salt.
2. She doesn't have any pepper.
3. She needs an onion.
4. ______
5. ______
6. ______
7. ______
8. ______
9. ______

B. STYLE: Audience

1 *Look again at the letters from Confused Shopper and Mr. Green in Reading One in Section 3A on page 123. Then discuss these questions with a partner.*

1. Why did Confused Shopper and Mr. Green write these letters?
2. How do these letters seem different from letters that you would write to a friend?

Confused Shopper wrote to Mr. Green for one specific reason: to get answers to questions about organic produce. Mr. Green wrote to give Confused Shopper those answers. So their letters are very different from letters you would write to a friend.

When Mr. Green wrote to Confused Shopper, he was also writing to the people who read the newspaper where his letters appear. Confused Shopper and the newspaper readers are the audience for Mr. Green's letters.

Audience, Content, and Tone

In any kind of writing, **audience** refers to the people who read what you write. What you say—**content**—and how you say it—the **tone**—will depend on your audience.

Tips on content:

- Write about what your audience needs to know.
- Write about what will interest your audience.
- Write about what will be appropriate for your audience. A letter to a friend will probably be about everyday, personal things. A letter to a boss will probably be about professional things only.

Tips on tone:

- A letter to a close friend may have a lot of slang and may sound very casual. A letter to a teacher or a boss will not use any slang and will be more formal.
- When you write to a friend, you can express negative emotions like anger. When you write to a teacher, to a boss, or to people you don't know, you should avoid expressing these emotions directly.

2 *Mr. Green wrote magazine articles about organic food for three different magazines. Read the information about the three magazines.*

- *Mother's World* is a magazine for mothers. It gives advice on food, schools, and many other topics.
- *Garden Times* is for people who have homes with gardens and like to grow flowers and perhaps some fruits and vegetables for their families.
- *Farming News* is for professional farmers; it gives them the latest information about farming.

The following sentences come from the three magazine articles. The content of the three articles is very different, because the audiences are so different. Read each group of sentences and decide which magazine they come from. With a partner, discuss your answer.

1. Growing organic vegetables is not as hard as you think. In fact, it might be easier and more fun. Instead of using chemicals to keep out weeds and insects, try planting flowers that keep insects away from your vegetables.

   ____________________ magazine

2. Ten years ago, few people were willing to pay the higher prices for organic produce. But today you'll find that many people will spend more money to buy fruits and vegetables that are free of pesticides and herbicides.

   ____________________ magazine

3. Eating organic fruits and vegetables is one way to better health. Organic produce is healthy because it is grown naturally without any chemicals.

   ____________________ magazine

3 *You are writing two letters. In one letter, you are explaining to the manager of your school or office cafeteria why the cafeteria should serve organic produce. In the other letter, you tell a friend who always eats organic food about the cafeteria. Read the following sentences and decide which letter they are from. (Remember to think about content and tone.) Write* ***manager*** *or* ***friend****. Discuss your choices with a partner. The first one has been done for you.*

__manager__________ 1. Organic produce is healthier because it is grown without chemicals.

__________________ 2. Isn't that crazy—no organic produce!

_______________ 3. I am certain that the cafeteria will attract more customers if it decides to serve organic produce.

_______________ 4. Thank you for considering my request for organic produce.

_______________ 5. Take care. I'll see you soon!

_______________ 6. You wouldn't believe the problems I'm having with that bad cafeteria.

_______________ 7. I am writing to bring a problem to your attention: The cafeteria does not serve organic produce.

_______________ 8. More and more people are buying organic produce.

_______________ 9. Many people believe that organic produce tastes better than other produce.

_______________ 10. I've got to say, I really miss my Mom's home cooking.

4 *On a separate piece of paper, complete your letter to the cafeteria manager. Use the sentences above and some sentences of your own. (Begin the letter with "Dear Sir or Madam," and close it with "Sincerely yours," and your name.) [For more explanation on letter writing, see Unit 4, Section 3A, page 76.]*

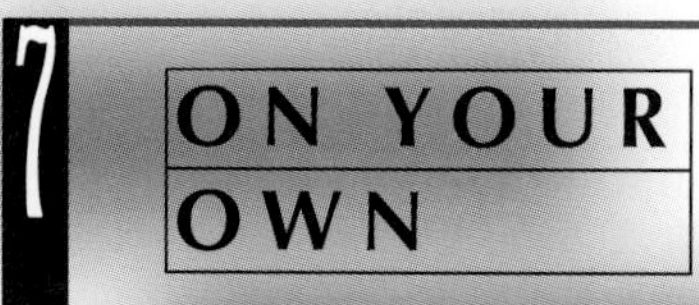

7 ON YOUR OWN

A. WRITING TOPICS

Choose one of the following topics. Use some of the vocabulary, grammar, and style that you learned in this unit.

1. Think of a recipe that you like and know how to cook. Write the recipe. You can use the recipe from exercise 4 in Section 6A, page 133, as a model. First list the ingredients. Then write the directions for cooking. (The directions should be in the imperative; that is, use the base form of the verb.) Be sure to pay attention to count nouns and non-count nouns.

2. Write a letter to Mr. Green. (You might want to read the letter by Confused Shopper from Reading Two again.) In your letter, first tell about something you have seen in stores and don't understand. Then ask one or two questions about it. For example, maybe you have seen tomatoes that say "vine-ripened." But you thought all tomatoes grow on vines. What does "vine-ripened" mean?

   Compare letters with those of other students. As a class, answer as many of the questions as you can.

3. Imagine that you must write a short explanation (1 to 3 paragraphs) of organic food for an article in a children's magazine. The children who read the magazine are 8 to 12 years old. Most of them live in big cities, and most are not familiar with organic food. Before you write the explanation, think of your audience and of the content and tone that would be best. What will interest your readers? What will they need to know?

   After you write your explanation, compare it to those of other students. Discuss how your audience made a difference for what your wrote.

B. FIELDWORK

Work in a group of three or four. Write a produce shopping guide. This shopping guide will help people shop for produce. Follow these steps:

1. As a group, choose five fruits and vegetables to research. Check with other groups to avoid repeating the same fruits and vegetables.

   ____

   ____

   ____

   ____

   ____

2. Together, buy two of each of your fruits and vegetables—one that is organic and one that is nonorganic. You may have to go to two different stores. Be sure to write down the cost of each piece (by the piece or by the pound). Bring all ten pieces of produce to class.

3. With your group, study your produce. Compare the organic produce with the regular produce. Look at the fruits and vegetables. Touch them. Smell them. Taste them. (Remember to wash them first.) Discuss these questions for each of the five kinds of produce:

   Can you tell the difference between the organic and the nonorganic produce? Do they look the same? Do they smell the same? Do they taste the same? Do they cost the same?

4. Complete a chart like the following for each of the five kinds of produce you researched. Fill in the price for the organic and nonorganic produce. For each of the other categories (color, taste, smell, and feel), check (√) organic or nonorganic—the one that is better in this category. Then write a short recommendation. For this kind of produce, do you think people should buy organic, nonorganic, or either one?

KIND OF PRODUCE: ______________________

	Organic	**Nonorganic**
Color		
Taste		
Smell		
Feel		
Price		

Recommendation: ______________________

____

____

5. Put all the charts together to make a produce shopping guide.

UNIT 8

A CHEAP WAY TO TRAVEL

1 APPROACHING THE TOPIC

A. PREDICTING

Look at the picture. Discuss your answers to the questions.

1. Where are these travelers?
2. What kind of trip are they taking?
3. Look at the title of this unit. What cheap ways to travel do you think this unit will mention?

B. SHARING INFORMATION

What are some ways that you know of to travel without spending very much money? Fill in the lists of "dos" and "don'ts." In small groups, discuss your lists. The first one has been done for you.

If you want to travel cheaply. . .

DO

1. have picnics
2. __________
3. __________
4. __________
5. __________

DON'T

1. eat in expensive restaurants every day
2. __________
3. __________
4. __________
5. __________

2 PREPARING TO READ

A. BACKGROUND

Work with a partner. Look at the advertisements for airline tickets. Then discuss the questions that follow.

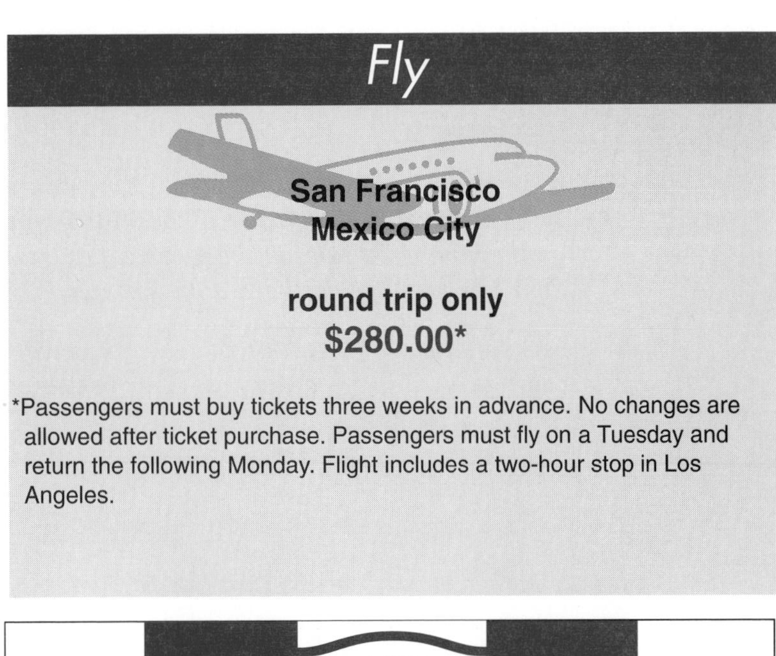

Fly
San Francisco
Mexico City
round trip only
$280.00*
*Passengers must buy tickets three weeks in advance. No changes are allowed after ticket purchase. Passengers must fly on a Tuesday and return the following Monday. Flight includes a two-hour stop in Los Angeles.

A.

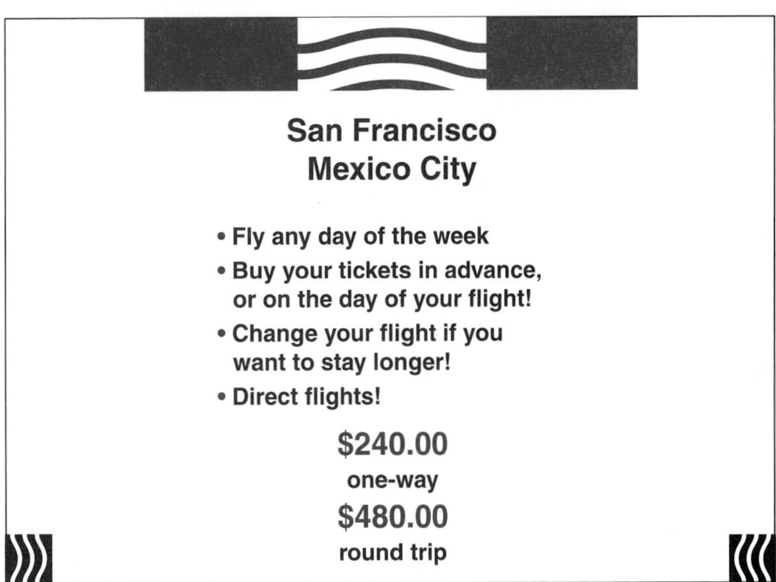

San Francisco
Mexico City
• Fly any day of the week
• Buy your tickets in advance, or on the day of your flight!
• Change your flight if you want to stay longer!
• Direct flights!
$240.00
one-way
$480.00
round trip

B.

1. In what ways are these tickets different? ______________________________

____

2. Which ticket might be best for travelers like the ones in the picture in Section 1A? ______________________________

3. Which ticket might be best for your next vacation? ________________

B. VOCABULARY FOR COMPREHENSION

The passenger in the picture is checking in for her flight. Write the words on the numbered rules in the picture. (Two words have the same meaning.) The first one has been done for you.

backpack	carry-on bag	luggage	round-trip ticket
baggage	counter	~~package~~	signs

3 READING ONE: Low on Cash? Try Paris for a Vacation!

A. INTRODUCING THE TOPIC

Look at the title and read the first two paragraphs. Try to answer this question:

Why was Brian wearing so many clothes?

Read the whole text and see if your guess is right.

Low on cash?[1] Try Paris for a Vacation!

1 Brian arrived at the San Francisco airport two hours before the flight to Paris. He was wearing three shirts, a jacket, two pairs of socks, a pair of shorts, and two pairs of jeans. He was carrying one small backpack, which was very full, but he didn't have any other luggage. Brian needed to meet a man named Tony before he checked in for his flight. He found Tony near the Air France counter. Tony gave him a round-trip ticket and a small package.

2 "Give this package to Jean-Paul at the airport in Paris. Jean-Paul is very tall with short, blond, curly hair. He will have a sign with your name on it. I think you can find him easily," Tony said. "You don't have any luggage, right?"

3 "Only this backpack," Brian answered. "You said I could bring one carry-on bag."

4 "That's right. One carry-on bag is fine. Have a good trip."

5 "Thanks."

6 Is Brian a criminal? Not at all. He is an air courier. And he paid only $110 for the round-trip ticket to Paris. Air couriers get cheap airline tickets because they take important packages and papers to foreign countries. Businesses sometimes need to get packages and papers to people in foreign countries by the next day. Often, the only way they can do this is to use an air-courier company. It is not cheap for a business to send a package with an air courier, but it is quick. Instead of luggage, couriers often

[1] *Low on cash:* an informal way to say "very little money"

have packages for the air-courier company. Sometimes the packages get checked, and sometimes the air-couriers carry them so that they don't lose time waiting for baggage to be unloaded off the airplane. Whether the packages are checked or carried on, they go through customs quickly with an air courier. In contrast, if a package is sent in the mail, it can stay in customs for many days while customs officials decide if it needs to be taxed.

7 Every year about 80,000 people worldwide travel as air couriers. The number of tickets for courier travel is growing by about 10 percent a year. Many people like traveling this way because the tickets are so cheap. However, air-courier travel has some disadvantages. You usually can't check any luggage. You also need to be very flexible about your travel plans because you can only travel when and where a business needs you to go.

8 Air-courier travel obviously isn't for everyone. But if you have only a little cash, can be flexible about your plans, and don't mind wearing the same clothes for a week, it can be a great way to take a vacation!

B. READING FOR MAIN IDEAS

Circle the best answer for each question.

1. Why do people want to be air couriers?

a. They want to find a good job.

b. They want to get cheap airline tickets.

c. They want to send packages quickly.

2. What is difficult about being an air courier?

a. You can't take much luggage, and you can travel only when a business needs an air courier.

b. There are fewer air-courier tickets every year, and travelers have difficulties finding tickets.

c. You need to arrive at the airport earlier than other passengers, and you need to go through customs.

3. Why do businesses use air couriers?

a. It is easy to find couriers.

b. It is cheap to send a package with an air courier.

c. Packages arrive quickly with air couriers.

C. READING FOR DETAILS

All of the following statements are false. Change a word or phrase in each statement to make it true. The first one has been done for you.

1. Brian wore ~~one pair~~ two pairs of jeans.
2. He arrived at the airport three hours before his flight to Paris.
3. Brian had a lot of luggage.
4. Tony gave Brian a large envelope.
5. Jean-Paul is very tall with long, blond, curly hair.
6. Brian paid only $110 for a one-way ticket to Paris.
7. Air couriers often can check luggage.
8. If a package is sent by mail, it can be on a ship for many days.

D. READING BETWEEN THE LINES

Decide if the sentences are true or false. Write **T** *or* **F** *next to each sentence. Then discuss your answers with a partner.*

_____ **1.** Brian is probably traveling on business.

_____ **2.** Jean-Paul works for the air-courier company.

_____ **3.** Air couriers usually can take only one set of clothes.

_____ **4.** Items in an air courier's luggage don't get taxed.

_____ **5.** Air couriers are more necessary today than they were years ago.

4 READING TWO: An E-Mail Mix-Up

A. EXPANDING THE TOPIC

Read the information and e-mails. Then answer the questions that follow with a partner.

Hiroshi is a student in New York. He wants to go to France for spring break to visit his friend in Paris. In the newspaper, he saw an ad for economy-class tickets to Paris. A round-trip ticket costs $599. The ticket has to be purchased three weeks in advance. A person can change the ticket later, but has to pay extra money to do this. Hiroshi isn't worried about buying the ticket in advance or about changing it. But he is afraid that he won't have enough money for the ticket. He has $800 to spend on the whole trip. To find out about other tickets, he contacted a travel agent by e-mail.

From: jones@travelworld.com
Date: Tue, 28 Oct 09:14:32
To: hsato@nyu.edu
Subject: Tickets to Paris

1 Thank you for contacting Travelworld about tickets for your trip to Paris. We can certainly find a comfortable way for you to travel from New York to Paris for the amount of money you are prepared to spend. Here are a couple of the possibilities:

2 Air France first class is very comfortable. The round-trip ticket, JFK <—> Paris, costs $8,190.00. The service is excellent, with gourmet food and wine. Seats are comfortable and give you plenty of space. You get limousine service between the airports and your home or destination in New York and Paris.

3 The Air France Concorde flight is, of course, the fastest way to travel to France. The round-trip ticket costs $8,567.00, and it is certainly worth the extra money. The entire Concorde flight is always first class, so you will have all the benefits described above. The added benefit is that the Concorde takes only 3 hours and 45 minutes to arrive (the regular flight takes about 6 1/2 hours). This would be a good chance for you to take the Concorde. It goes only between New York and Paris, and New York and London!

4 Let me know if I can help you make your decision.

Kerry Jones

On Tue, 28 Oct, you wrote:
>To: jones@travelworld.com
>Sender: hsato@nyu.edu
>Re: Tickets to Paris

5 >I would like some information about tickets to Paris for spring break (the
>last week in March). I would like to stay for one week. I read that a regular
>economy ticket costs $600, but I would like information about other fares.
>I have about $8000 to spend.

1. Why was the travel agent's e-mail surprising to Hiroshi? ___________

____

2. Why did she give him information about the most expensive flights?

____

B. LINKING READINGS ONE AND TWO

1 *Use the information in Readings One and Two to fill in the advantages and disadvantages of each kind of travel.*

TYPE OF TRAVEL	ADVANTAGES	DISADVANTAGES
Air courier		
Economy class		
Concorde		
First class		

❷ *Read about the following travelers and decide in small groups which type of ticket might be best for each one.*

1. Marguerite is eighty-one years old. She lives in England, but her daughters and grandchildren live in California. The last time she visited them was fifteen years ago. She would really like to go for another visit, but she has very stiff legs and hips, so it is impossible for her to sit in a regular airplane seat.

   ____

2. Alexandra, who is ten, is flying from Chicago to New York to spend the summer with her aunt. It is her first time flying alone. Her parents are going to take her to the airport, and her aunt will pick her up in New York.

   ____

3. Nicole A. Hughes, president of Hughes High Fashion Clothing Company, needs to be in Paris for a fashion show on Saturday evening, but she also has a very important client coming to New York who is expecting to meet her for dinner on Sunday.

   ____

4. Brock is a young filmmaker in Los Angeles. He wants to make an educational film about the Hmong people who live in Southeast Asia.

   ____

5. Larry and his girlfriend are both teachers in Miami. They really want to go together to London to visit Larry's cousins for three weeks in the summer. They have a month of vacation time.

   ____

5 REVIEWING LANGUAGE

A. EXPLORING LANGUAGE

Read the following sentences. Where might you be most likely to hear them? Write the letter in the correct column. The first one has been done for you.

a. If you have more than three liters of alcohol, you must pay a tax.

b. Are you interested in the round trip?

c. Please put your carry-on bags under the seat or in the overhead compartment.

d. How many bags do you want to check?

e. Please open your luggage for me to see.

f. This way is a little more expensive, but I think you will find it is worth it.

g. Did you pack your own bags?

h. How flexible are your traveling dates?

i. Your flight is leaving from gate 38. Follow the signs.

j. Here are your tickets. Remember to check in at least 90 minutes before the flight.

k. I'm sorry, but you'll have to check your backpack.

AT THE TRAVEL AGENT	AT THE AIRLINE COUNTER	ON THE FLIGHT	IN CUSTOMS
			a

B. WORKING WITH WORDS

When Brian arrived in Paris, he found Jean-Paul easily. Complete their conversation with the words below.

carry-on bag	check in for	flight	luggage
check	disadvantage	it's worth it	package

JEAN-PAUL: Welcome to Paris! How was your (1) ________________?

BRIAN: Oh, it was fine, but I am ready to take off some of these clothes.

JEAN-PAUL: Yes. . . It is summer here, you know. . .

BRIAN: I know, but I needed to bring some clothes, and I couldn't fit everything into one (2) ________________.

JEAN-PAUL: Oh, I see. Yes, that is a (3) ________________ of air-courier travel. You can't bring much (4) ________________.

BRIAN: You're right, but (5) ________________. I don't mind being uncomfortable for a few hours if I can get a cheap ticket.

JEAN-PAUL: Do you have the (6) ________________?

BRIAN: I hope so. . . yes, here it is.

JEAN-PAUL: Great. Thank you.

BRIAN: Thank you! Do I need to meet you here when I go back to the States?

JEAN-PAUL: No. Your job is finished. You can just (7) ________________ your flight like a regular passenger.

BRIAN: Can I (8) ____________ some luggage, too?

JEAN-PAUL: Of course.

BRIAN: Great! Then I don't have to wear everything on the plane!

6 SKILLS FOR EXPRESSION

A. GRAMMAR: Modals: *Can* and *Could* for Ability and Possibility

1 *Before Brian bought an air-courier ticket, he called an air-courier company to ask some questions. Read the conversation between Brian and a receptionist at the company. Underline all the uses of* ***can, can't, could,*** *and* ***couldn't****. With a partner, answer the questions that follow.*

BRIAN:	I want to fly to Paris as an air courier. Can I ask you a couple of questions?
RECEPTIONIST:	Sure.
BRIAN:	Do I need any special training to be an air courier? Also, I can't speak French. Is that OK?
RECEPTIONIST:	No, you don't need special training, and you don't need to speak French. If you can arrive at the airport two hours before the flight and bring an envelope to someone at the other end, you can be an air courier.
BRIAN:	Last year, when I traveled with a regular economy-class ticket, I could travel only on certain days, and I couldn't change my ticket after I bought it. What happens if I go as an air courier?
RECEPTIONIST:	It works the same way. In fact, if you go as an air courier, you need to be even more flexible about your plans. . . .

1. What does *can* mean?
2. What is the difference between *can* and *can't*?
3. What is the difference between *can* and *could*?

Focus on Grammar

See *Can* and *Could* in *Focus on Grammar, Basic.*

Modals: *Can* and *Could*

We use ***can*** to express possibility or ability in the present. ***Can't*** is the negative of *can.*	I **can** speak French. = I am able to speak French. No, you **can't** fly tomorrow. = No, it's impossible for you to fly tomorrow.
We use ***could*** to express ability or possibility in the past. ***Couldn't*** is the negative of *could.*	Last time I traveled, I **could** buy cheap airline tickets in advance. = Last time I traveled, it was possible for me to buy cheap airline tickets in advance. Last time I traveled, I **couldn't** change my ticket after buying it. = Last time I traveled, it wasn't possible to change my ticket after buying it.
Can and *could* are also used to make polite requests.	**Could** I please ask you some questions? **Can** I borrow your pen?

Always use the base form of the verb with *can, can't, could,* and *couldn't.*

Can/Can't Could/Couldn't		**Base Form of Verb**	
Can	I	ask	you some questions?
I couldn't		change	my ticket after buying it.

2 *Complete the paragraph with* **can, can't, could,** *or* **couldn't** *and the base form of the verb. Pay attention to present and past time.*

Last year, Hung went on vacation to Hong Kong. He flew as an air courier. He was very happy with the price of the ticket. But his ticket was non-refundable. He ________________ it after he bought it. Usually he
1. (change)

flies as a regular passenger, and his tickets are refundable. If he wants, he ________________ them.
2. (change)

When Hung went to Hong Kong, he ________________ any luggage
3. (check)

because he was an air courier. He ________________ only one small
4. (bring)

carry-on bag. But when he flies as a regular passenger, he ________________ as many bags as he wants.
5. (check)

When he traveled as an air courier, he ________________ exactly
6. (travel)

when he wanted. He ________________ only when the courier company
7. (travel)

needed him.

As a regular passenger, Hung ________________ any time he wants,
8. (travel)

and he ________________ his tickets months in advance. He likes to
9. (buy)

travel as a regular passenger—but he doesn't like the cost!

3 *Write sentences about which kind of travel is/was possible/not possible for the following travelers. Use* **can, can't,** *or* **could** *and the words and phrases that follow. Most items have more than one possible answer. The first one has been done for you.*

VERBS	KINDS OF TRAVEL
go	as an air courier
fly	economy class
travel	first class
	by Concorde jet

1. Alice isn't sure when she will return from Casablanca.

   She can't go as an air courier because she's not flexible.

2. Wen is a basketball player. He is seven feet tall and he has very long legs.

   ____

3. Janet has lots of money. She wants to go to London.

   ____

4. Elizabeth had very little money to spend on her airplane ticket.

   ____

5. Robin needed to make a reservation two months before Christmas.

   ____

6. Hal needs to take many gifts to his relatives in Norway.

   ____

7. Nicole is afraid of being on an airplane for more than four hours. She needs to fly from New York to London.

   ____

B. STYLE: Connecting Sentences with *And* and *But*

1 *Look at the pairs of sentences. Decide which sentences explain advantages about first-class and air-courier travel and which sentences explain disadvantages. Check (√) the appropriate column.*

	Advantages	Disadvantages
First-Class Travel		
First class has lots of space.	________	________
First class has very good food.	________	________
Air-Courier Travel		
Air-courier travel is cheap.	________	________
Air couriers can't bring much luggage.	________	________

Connect each pair of sentences into one. Use ***and*** *or* ***but.***

Connecting Sentences with *And* and *But*

The connector word ***and*** connects sentences that have similar ideas—for example, two sentences about advantages.

First class has lots of space, **and** it has very good food.

(advantage) *, and* (advantage)

The connector word ***but*** connects sentences that have contrasting ideas—for example, a sentence about an advantage and a sentence about a disadvantage.

Air-courier travel is cheap, **but** air couriers can't bring much luggage.

(advantage) *, but* (disadvantage)

When you connect two sentences with *and* or *but*, use a comma (,) between the ideas.

Air-courier travel is cheap**,** but air couriers can't bring much luggage.

When the subject of both sentences is the same, use a pronoun as the subject in the second sentence.

First class has lots of space, and ~~first class~~ it has very good food.

2 *Fill in the blanks with the correct connector word (**and** or **but**). Add the correct punctuation. The first one has been done for you.*

1. Brian had a lot of time for his vacation, <u>but</u> he didn't have a lot of money.
2. Brian loves living in San Francisco ______ he misses his friends in Paris.
3. A Concorde jet will get you to London very quickly ______ there is only one Concorde flight each day.
4. Airline seats often seem uncomfortable ______ airline food often seems bad.
5. If you want to save money, you should call Dirt Cheap Travel ______ if you have plenty of money, you can call any travel agent.
6. Brian couldn't check bags to Paris ______ he can check bags back to San Francisco.
7. Air-courier travel is cheap ______ the work is easy.

3 *Think about a recent trip you took somewhere. What were some advantages and disadvantages? Write sentences using **and** and **but**.*

Example:

My flight to Singapore was very long, but the people were very nice.

1. ______________________, but ______________________
2. ______________________, and ______________________
3. ____
4. ____
5. ____
6. ____

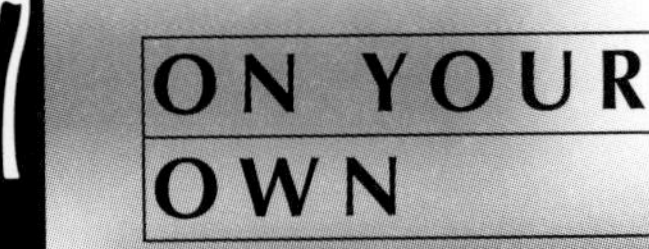

7 ON YOUR OWN

A. WRITING TOPICS

Choose one of the following topics. Write one or two paragraphs. Use some of the vocabulary, grammar, and style that you learned in this unit.

1. Look back at Section 4A, page 146. Write an e-mail to Hiroshi. Explain his mistake to him. Then give him some advice about ways to save money when he travels.

2. Describe a very cheap trip that you took. It doesn't have to be a trip on an airplane. How did you travel? Was it worth it?

3. Think about the ways of traveling in the area you live in. Describe the advantages and disadvantages of two kinds of travel (not air travel).

B. FIELDWORK

In small groups, research some inexpensive ways to travel. When you finish, share what you learned with the other students in your class. Follow these steps:

1. Ask students at your school: Where do you like to go for vacation? Use their answers to help you choose a popular place to research. (Each group should choose a different place.)

2. Get information about three ways to travel to this place. You can...
   - read the travel section of the newspaper.
   - talk to travel agents on the phone or in person.
   - do research on the Internet.

3. Fill out the following chart with information collected in your research. Then as a class, discuss and compare the different ways to travel to different popular vacation places.

INEXPENSIVE WAYS TO TRAVEL TO ___________

Transportation (plane, bus, train, other)			
Cost			
Advantages			
Disadvantages			
Phone number to call for reservations			

UNIT 9

THE WINTER BLUES

1 APPROACHING THE TOPIC

A. PREDICTING

Look at the picture. Discuss your answers to the questions.

1. This woman is not really sick. Why is she still in bed at noon?

2. What ideas do you have about why she might feel the way she does?

B. SHARING INFORMATION

Read the dictionary definitions for **depression.** *In small groups, discuss the questions.*

de•pres•sion /di′preshən/ ***n.*** **1.** a feeling or mood of sadness. **2.** a medical condition that makes you so unhappy that you cannot live a normal life

1. How are the two definitions of depression different?
2. Which kind of depression is more serious?
3. Someone is depressed in the sense of definition 1. What do you think he or she can do to feel better?
4. Someone is depressed in the sense of definition 2. What do you think he or she can do to feel better?

2 PREPARING TO READ

A. BACKGROUND

Read the passage about depression, then answer the true/false questions that follow.

Depressed is a word that can cause some confusion and misunderstandings. A student who receives a "D" on a test might say, "Oh, I'm so depressed," when he sees his grade. But then, an hour later, he is playing Frisbee with his friends and laughing. We get so used to hearing people say, "I'm depressed" in this casual way that we sometimes forget that *depressed* can also refer to a very serious medical condition.

About 10–20 percent of people have the more serious kind of depression (also called "clinical depression"[1]) sometime in their lives. Unlike the student with the "D," people who are clinically depressed don't forget about their depression. Their "low feeling" is not a

[1] In the rest of this unit, the words *depressed* and *depression* refer to clinical depression.

temporary mood. They often find it very difficult to work and concentrate. There are many reasons for this type of depression, and there are many ways to help people who have it. People who think they may be clinically depressed should see their doctors.

Decide if the sentences are true or false. Write **T** *or* **F** *next to each sentence.*

_____ **1.** A depressed mood usually goes away easily.

_____ **2.** If someone says, "I'm depressed," you should take him or her to the doctor immediately.

_____ **3.** If a person feels depressed for a long time, he or she should probably see a doctor.

_____ **4.** People get clinically depressed because they don't do well in school.

B. VOCABULARY FOR COMPREHENSION

Read the following story about Valerie. Try to guess the meanings of the underlined words.

Valerie <u>suffers</u> from depression. She doesn't know what <u>causes</u> her depression. She doesn't know what to do about it. Movies, parties, and other fun things don't seem to <u>affect</u> the way she feels.

For a long time, Valerie didn't know that she was <u>depressed</u>. She just thought that she was a naturally sad person. When she told her doctor about it, she found out that she had many of the <u>symptoms</u> of depression. She usually <u>lacked</u> energy, she sometimes stayed in bed for whole days at a time, and she often didn't feel like eating.

Valerie's doctor told her that depression is a <u>common</u> problem, one that he sees all the time. And he helped her choose the right <u>treatment</u>. She is taking some medicine that helps her feel less depressed. In addition, once a week she talks to a <u>psychiatrist</u> about herself and her problems.

Complete the sentences about Matthew, Valerie's friend, with the words in the list that follows. Matthew is not depressed. He has another problem.

affects	causes	common	depressed
lacks	psychiatrist	suffers	symptoms
treatments			

1. Matthew ________________ from headaches and backaches.
2. He knows that drinking too much coffee ________________ some of his headaches.
3. He notices that when he ________________ sleep, his headaches and backaches are worse.
4. He asked his doctor about ________________ for his headaches and backaches.
5. The doctor said, "I can give you some aspirin, or send you to a specialist, but they won't help you. Headaches, backaches, too much coffee, and not enough sleep are ________________ of a workaholic. The problem is in your mind, not your body."
6. "Oh. Do you think I might need to see a ________________?" Matthew asked.
7. "I don't think you need to see any more doctors. You just work too much. You need to work less! That's all. This is a ________________ problem these days for young people."
8. Matthew knows that his work ________________ his health, but he can't stop working.
9. "I love my work," says Matthew. "If I stop working so much, I will get ________________!"

3

READING ONE: Seasonal Affect Disorder

A. INTRODUCING THE TOPIC

The following article is from a family medical guide—a book that people can use to get information about common medical conditions. Look at the boldfaced titles in the article. Then answer this question:

What kind of information do you expect to find in this article? (Put a **Y** next to the things you think you will find and an **N** next to the things you don't think you will find.)

_____ Information about reasons why people have SAD

_____ Definition of SAD

_____ Names of good doctors to see if you have SAD

_____ Stories about people who have SAD

_____ Information to help you know if you have SAD

_____ Information about what to do if you have SAD

Read the whole article. Then check your answers to the question above.

Seasonal Affect Disorder (SAD)

1 People who have SAD get depressed during the fall and winter. SAD seems to be much more common in some places than in others. For example, in the United States, less than 1 percent of the people in Florida, a southern state, have SAD, but 10–30 percent of the people in Alaska, a northern state, have it.

Cause

2 Doctors aren't exactly sure about what causes SAD, but they are beginning to understand it better. The cause of SAD might be emotional (for example, some people get depressed at Christmastime

because they miss their families); the cause might also be chemical. Scientists have found that some chemicals in our bodies are affected by bright outdoor light (more than 1,500 lux[1]). Bright light causes our bodies to make more of some chemicals and less of other chemicals. These chemicals affect our breathing, blood pressure, and body temperature.

Symptoms

3 The symptoms of SAD are almost the same as the symptoms of depression. The biggest difference is that depression can happen at any time of year, but SAD happens only during the fall and winter months, particularly in the far north and far south where there is less light in the winter. The most common symptoms include:

- sleeping more than usual
- having a bigger appetite than usual
- gaining or losing weight quickly
- lacking energy
- thinking about death
- not wanting to be with other people

Treatment

4 The three most common treatments for SAD are light therapy, psychotherapy, and drug therapy.[2]

5 Light therapy is becoming the most common treatment for people with SAD. Sixty to 80 percent of SAD sufferers can feel better if bright light reaches their eyes every day. The light should be brighter than 2,500 lux, and the person with SAD should be near it for one-half to three hours per day in the morning. To get this light, a person with SAD can take walks outside on bright mornings or sit near a special bright light. The light should reach the eyes, but it should not be too close or it might hurt him or her. Light therapy is the most natural, cheapest, and easiest treatment for SAD, but some people don't have the time it requires.

6 Psychotherapy with a professional psychiatrist or psychologist is another common treatment for depression or SAD. In psychotherapy, the patient talks about problems that he or she is having that might be causing the depression. Psychotherapy is probably the best treatment for emotional causes of SAD or depression, but it can take a very long time, and it can be very expensive.

7 Antidepressant drugs, such as Prozac, are also a common treatment for SAD and depression. These drugs affect the chemicals in our brains. They make most people feel less depressed quickly, but many people can't take these drugs because they actually cause other problems, for example, stomach problems and sleeping problems.

---

[1] We use lux to measure how bright a light is. A sunny day is about 10,000 lux. A dining room is usually about 100 lux.

[2] If you think you suffer from depression or SAD, you should talk to your doctor. Your doctor can tell you about the best treatment for you.

B. READING FOR MAIN IDEAS

Choose the best ending for each sentence.

1. SAD is like . . .
a. a sad feeling.
b. depression in the winter or fall.
c. being very tired all the time.

2. The causes of SAD . . .
a. are 100 percent emotional.
b. might be emotional and chemical.
c. are unknown.

3. The symptoms of SAD are . . .
a. like the symptoms of depression.
b. different for everyone.
c. like the symptoms of a cold.

4. Treatments for SAD include . . .
a. light, psychotherapy and drugs.
b. sleeping and exercising.
c. losing weight and eating healthier food.

C. READING FOR DETAILS

Look at the article again. In the chart, write the types of treatments for SAD and list the advantages and disadvantages of each.

TYPE OF TREATMENT	ADVANTAGES	DISADVANTAGES
Light therapy	**1.** most natural **2.** **3.**	**1.** takes a lot of time
	1.	**1.** **2.**
	1.	**1.**

D. READING BETWEEN THE LINES

Decide if the sentences are true or false. Write **T** *or* **F** *next to each sentence. Then discuss your answers with the class.*

_____ **1.** People in Canada are more likely to have SAD than people in Mexico.

_____ **2.** Scientists have found the cause of SAD.

_____ **3.** If you have a bigger appetite than usual, you probably have SAD.

_____ **4.** Light therapy is a common treatment for depression.

_____ **5.** Lighting a lot of candles in the evening could help a person with SAD.

4 READING TWO: Sunrise and Sunset Times around the World

A. EXPANDING THE TOPIC

1 *Look at the map of the world and the places on the chart. Write the names of the places on the correct lines in the map.*

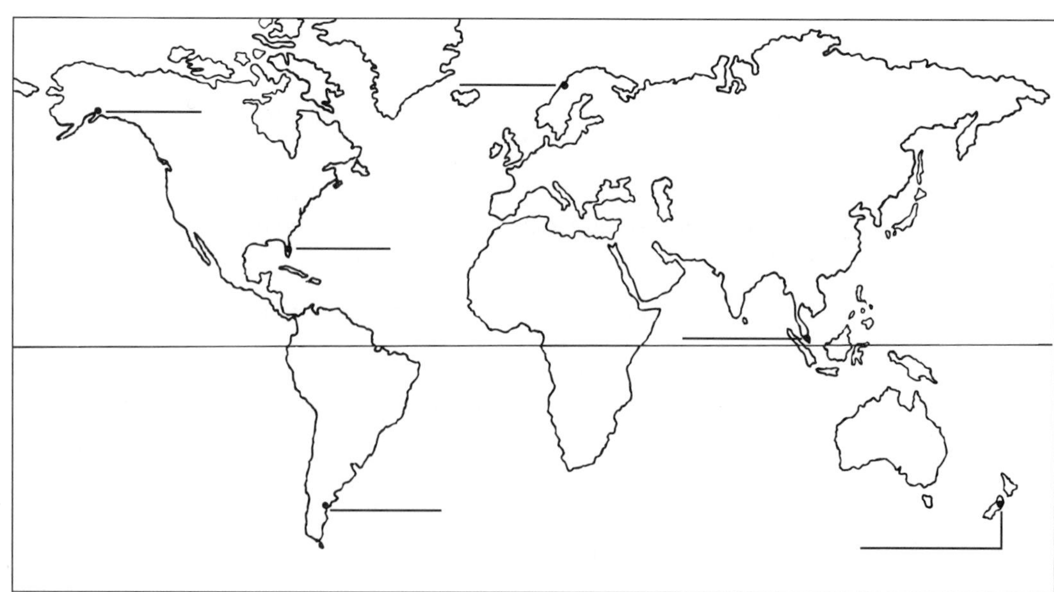

❷ *Look carefully at the chart. It gives the sunrise and sunset times for these places on January 1 and on July 1. Add your own town in the last space, and guess the sunrise and sunset times for it.*

❸ *Calculate the number of hours of sunlight in each place and fill in the chart with these numbers. The first one has been done for you.*

PLACE	JANUARY 1		HOURS OF DAYLIGHT	JULY 1		HOURS OF DAYLIGHT
	Sunrise	**Sunset**		**Sunrise**	**Sunset**	
Anchorage, Alaska (US)	10:13	15:53	5:40	04:28	22:38	
Orlando, Florida (US)	07:18	17:40		06:31	20:27	
Rørvik, Norway	10:06	14:02		01:16	22:50	
Puerto Santa Cruz, Argentina	03:36	19:51		07:39	15:49	
Christchurch, New Zealand	04:53	20:10		08:00	17:04	
Singapore	06:03	18:04		05:57	18:11	
(Your town)						

B. LINKING READINGS ONE AND TWO

Use the information from Readings One and Two to predict where SAD is common in January and July and where it is not common. Be prepared to explain your answers.

1. Do you think that SAD is common or not common in your town?

____

2. Of the places listed, the most common places for SAD in January are probably:

____

3. The most common place for SAD in July is probably:

____

4. The two places where SAD is probably rare are:

____

5. The two places where SAD is probably most common are:

____

6. Reading One gives two causes for SAD. Which cause are the numbers in the chart related to?

____

REVIEWING LANGUAGE

A. EXPLORING LANGUAGE

Read each pair of sentences. Change one or two words in the second sentence so that the sentences make sense together. Pay attention to the meanings of the underlined words. The first one has been done for you.

1. Scott has a high <u>temperature</u>. His forehead feels ~~cold~~ hot.
2. I don't think that the cat is <u>breathing</u>. It is probably alive.
3. My son has a huge <u>appetite</u>. He hates to eat.
4. Bob is trying <u>psychotherapy</u> to help him with his problem. He thinks that taking medicine will help.
5. Penny has <u>lost weight</u>. She looks fatter now.
6. The sun is really <u>bright</u> today. I think I need to take off my sunglasses.
7. Noriko and Masaki <u>gained weight</u> when they moved to the United States. I think they ate too many carrots.

8. Mr. McDonald suffers from high blood pressure. He should eat less salt and try to relax less.

9. Kim had to drop out of school because he was having emotional problems. I think that he should talk to a heart doctor.

10. Vanessa can't reach the teapot in her cupboard. Her husband, who is shorter than she is, always gets it when she needs it.

B. WORKING WITH WORDS

For each paragraph, find the group of words that fits. Then complete the paragraph with the correct words from that group.

affect — blood pressure — cause — emotions
appetite — depressed — gaining weight — lost weight
bright — suffers — symptoms — treatment
common — temperature — temperature — treatment

1. When we get worried, our _____________ often goes up. _____________ can _____________ our blood pressure, and stress can _____________ high blood pressure.

2. A normal, healthy person's _____________ is 98.6° F (37° C), but it is _____________ for a person to have a higher _____________ if he or she has a bad cold. A good _____________ is to put cold cloths on the person's head.

3. After Ellen's father died last year, she became very _____________. She didn't have any _____________, so she _____________. But last month she started talking to a psychotherapist. Now she is feeling better and she is _____________ again.

4. Jean thinks she _____________ from SAD because she never wants to go to work on days that aren't _____________ and sunny. But she doesn't have any other _____________ of SAD. I think the best _____________ for her problem is a new job!

6 SKILLS FOR EXPRESSION

A. GRAMMAR: Modal: *Should*

❶ *Alice has learned that she might have SAD, so she wants to try light therapy. Read the conversation between Alice and a salesperson at a lighting store. Answer the questions that follow.*

SALESPERSON:	OK, here is your 10,000 lux light. Do you know how to use it?
ALICE:	Well, my doctor told me a few things. He said I <u>should sit</u> near it for two hours every morning.
SALESPERSON:	That's right, and you <u>should sit</u> with the light next to your face. Remember, you <u>should see</u> the light, but you <u>shouldn't look</u> directly at it.
ALICE:	I won't. I don't want to hurt my eyes. That light is really bright. How close <u>should</u> I <u>sit</u>?
SALESPERSON:	About two to four feet away. You <u>shouldn't sit</u> too close.
ALICE:	Two to four feet. OK.
SALESPERSON:	OK, good luck. I hope it works for you!
ALICE:	I hope so too! Thanks.

1. Why do the speakers use *should* and *shouldn't* in their conversation?
2. What form of the verb do you see with *should* or *shouldn't*?

FOCUS ON GRAMMAR

See *Should* in *Focus on Grammar, Basic.*

Modals: *Should* and *Shouldn't*

Use ***should*** to give advice or say that something is a good idea.

You **should sit** two to four feet away from this light. = It's a good idea to sit two to four feet away from the light.

Use ***shouldn't*** to give advice or say that something isn't a good idea.

You **shouldn't look** directly at the light. = It's a bad idea to look directly at the light.

Always use the base form of the verb with *should* and *shouldn't.*

	Should(n't)	**Base Form of Verb**	
You	should	sit	two to four feet away from this light.
You	shouldn't	look	directly at the light.
How close	should I	sit?	

2 *Complete the sentences with* ***should*** *and* ***shouldn't*** *and the base form of the correct verb.*

eat	look	sleep	take
exercise	see	stay out	talk

1. You ________________ directly at a bright light.
2. People ________________ antidepressants if their doctors haven't told them to.
3. Jane has all of the symptoms of depression. She ________________ her doctor.
4. Bob is always tired because he goes out to bars almost every night. He ________________ more and he ________________ late every night.
5. Natalie is gaining too much weight. She ________________ more and she ________________ so much ice cream.
6. Jeremy is having serious problems in school, and he's fighting a lot with other kids. I think he ________________ to a psychiatrist.

3 *Write sentences with **should** and **shouldn't** to respond to the statements. Write at least two sentences with **should** and two sentences with **shouldn't**. The first one has been done for you.*

1. I have a terrible headache.

   You should take some aspirin.
2. I have all of the symptoms of the flu.

   ____
3. Dennis was playing football and hurt his back.

   ____
4. Richard and his girlfriend fight all of the time.

   ____
5. Eddie is losing weight very fast.

   ____

B. STYLE: Using Direct Speech

1 *Look at the conversation in Section 6A, exercise 1, again and read the text that follows. What is the difference between the two styles of writing a conversation?*

Alice was in the store buying a bright light to see if it would help with her SAD. The salesperson was very helpful. "OK, here is your 10,000 lux light. Do you know how to use it?" he asked.

"Well, my doctor told me a few things," Alice answered. "He said that I should sit near it for two hours every morning."

"That's right, and you should sit with the light next to your face," the salesperson said. "Remember, you should see the light, but you shouldn't look directly at it," he added.

"I won't. I don't want to hurt my eyes. That light really is bright. How close should I sit?" she asked.

"About two to four feet away," the salesperson answered.

Direct Speech

Often when we write about a conversation, we write exactly what the people say—that is, we use **direct speech**. Then the reader can hear the people talking. The exact words that a person says are called quotes. Use the verbs *say, ask, answer,* or *add* to introduce direct speech.

a. Use *say* for quotes which are not questions.

"That's right, and you should sit with the light next to your face," the salesperson **said**.

b. Use *add* when the speaker is adding information to something that he or someone else said just before.

"Remember, you should see the light, but you shouldn't look directly at it." he **added**.

c. Use *ask* for questions.

"How close should I sit?" she **asked**.

d. Use *answer* for answers.

"About two to four feet away," the salesperson **answered**.

Punctuation is important, too.

a. Always put quotation marks around the quote.

"Well, my doctor told me a few things,**"** Alice answered.

b. Put a comma between a quote and the main subject and verb of the sentence.

"Well, my doctor told me a few things**,**" Alice answered.

OR

Alice answered**,** "Well, my doctor told me a few things."

c. If the quote is a question, always use a question mark at the end of the quote, and before the quotation mark.	"Do you know how to use it**?**" he asked. OR He asked**,** "Do you know how to use it**?**"
Each time you begin a new quote from a different person, you need to start a new paragraph.	"I won't. I don't want to hurt my eyes. That light is really bright. How close should I sit?" she asked. "About two to four feet away," the salesperson answered.

2 *Joe is telling his friend about trying to make a doctor's appointment. Add the missing punctuation to the text. The first one has been done for you.*

I called to make an appointment at the doctor's yesterday. The receptionist answered the phone and asked, "Can I help you?"

So I answered Yes, I need to see Dr. Fong today

That's not possible she said. Dr. Fong doesn't have any free appointments for three weeks

Well, what should I do I asked. I need to see her right away

What exactly is the problem she asked.

I am always sleepy and I feel depressed I said to her. Maybe I need some antidepressant drugs I added.

3 *Complete the conversation between Joe and the receptionist with the correct verbs. The first one has been done for you.*

added answered asked said

"Well, is this really an emergency?" the receptionist (1) asked .

"Yes, it's an emergency!" I (2) ______________. I was getting angry.

"OK, you can come in at 4:20," she (3) ______________. "And don't be late," she (4) ______________. "The doctor has another patient at 4:30."

"I'll be on time, I promise," I (5) ______________. "Thank you very much."

"You're welcome," she (6) ______________.

4 *It is 4:30 and Joe is in Dr. Fong's office. On a separate piece of paper, rewrite the following conversation using direct speech. There is more than one way to rewrite the conversation. Finish it by adding some advice to Dr. Fong's last quote.*

DR. FONG:	So how are you doing?
JOE:	Oh, not too well. I think I need some anti-depressants. I'm always so tired these days. I can't get up in the morning. I usually don't have an appetite. I think I am depressed.
DR. FONG:	Hmm. How many hours of sleep do you usually get?
JOE:	Oh, about five. I like to watch late-night TV. I go to bed around two o'clock in the morning.
DR. FONG:	And what do you eat when you do feel like eating?
JOE:	Usually some cookies and a cup of strong coffee—I really like cookies, and the coffee helps to wake me up.
DR. FONG:	I think your problem might not be depression. I'm going to suggest something else to you. You should ________________ ________________ ________________

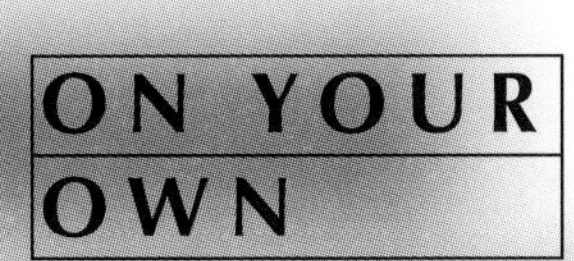

7 ON YOUR OWN

A. WRITING TOPICS

Choose one of the following topics. Write one or two paragraphs. Use some of the vocabulary, grammar, and style that you learned in this unit.

1. Write about a time you had a problem and asked for advice from a friend. Write about the discussion you had. What kind of advice did your friend give you? Was it good advice?

2. Do you know anyone who might be depressed? What makes you think he or she is depressed? If this person asks you for advice, what will you tell him or her?

3. Are your moods in the winter different from your moods in the summer? When do you feel saddest? What do you think you should and shouldn't do when you feel low?

B. FIELDWORK

Many depressed people don't know that they can get help. Make a brochure to help other students learn about depression. (See the following example.)

1. Work in a small group. To get information for your brochure, go to a local health clinic, public health agency, student health center, or library. If you think that SAD is common in your community, include information about SAD.

2. Write your brochure. In this brochure, you should answer the following questions:

   What is depression?

   How do I know if I might have it? (What are the symptoms?)

   What should I do if I think I am depressed?

3. Make sure that you get a classmate and a teacher to read your brochure before you give it to anyone else to read. Remember, depression is a very serious illness, so it is important to give correct information.

4. Share your brochure with the class.

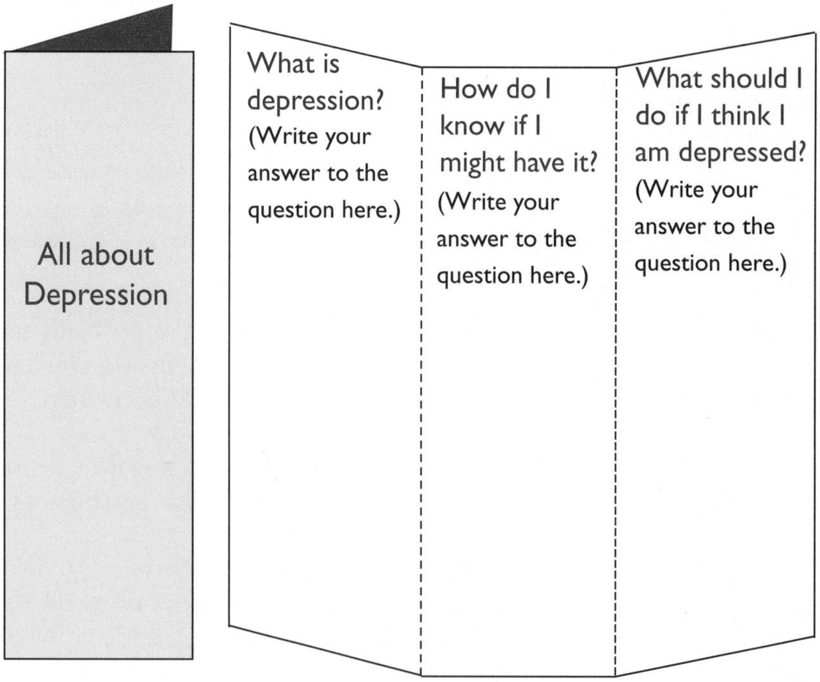

All about Depression
What is depression? (Write your answer to the question here.)
How do I know if I might have it? (Write your answer to the question here.)
What should I do if I think I am depressed? (Write your answer to the question here.)

UNIT 10

Developing Your Psychic Ability

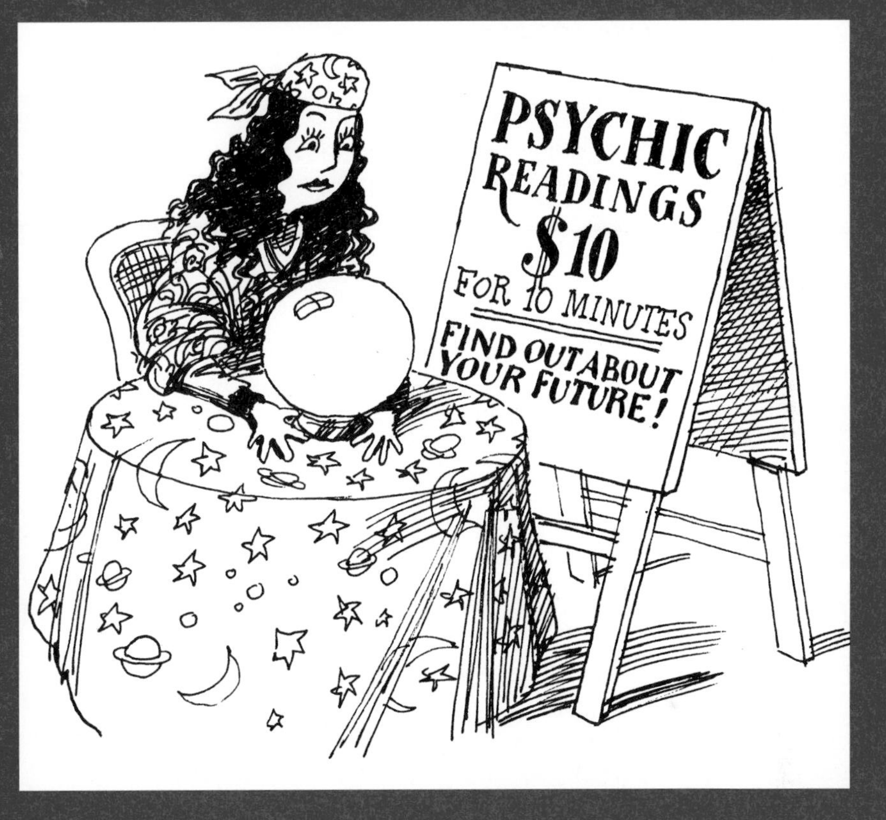

1 APPROACHING THE TOPIC

A. PREDICTING

Look at the picture and at the title of the unit. Discuss your answers to the questions.

1. How does this woman predict the future? Do you think she is able to predict the future? Why or why not?
2. Would you pay this woman $10 to tell you about your future? Why or why not?
3. What is psychic ability?

B. SHARING INFORMATION

Read the following statements. How much do you agree or disagree? Circle the number that gives your opinion. Then discuss your answers with a partner.

STRONGLY AGREE	AGREE	DISAGREE	STRONGLY DISAGREE	
1	2	3	4	**a.** Some people can predict the future.
1	2	3	4	**b.** Sometimes people can communicate without speaking or looking at each other.
1	2	3	4	**c.** Dreams can tell us things that we don't know.
1	2	3	4	**d.** Everyone has some psychic ability.
1	2	3	4	**e.** If an old friend calls while you are thinking about him or her one day, it is just a lucky chance.

2 PREPARING TO READ

A. BACKGROUND

Read the following text and discuss your answers to the questions with a partner.

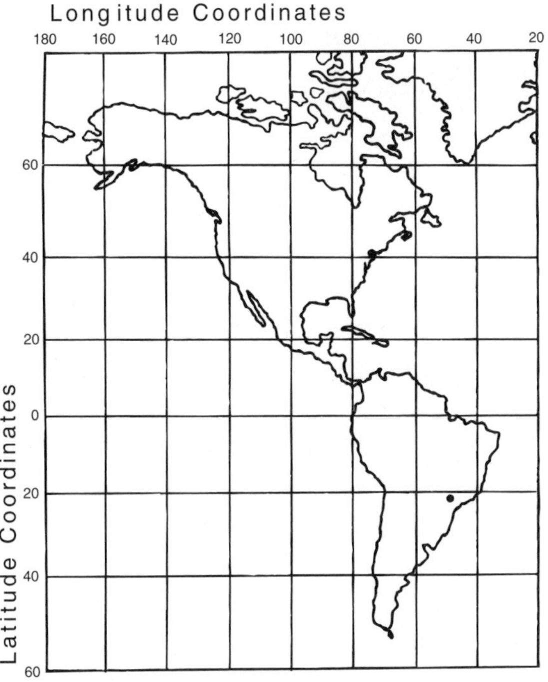

Is psychic ability real? Many people, including scientists, have asked this question. In one experiment, scientists told some psychics the longitude and latitude coordinates of a place, and asked the psychics to describe the place. The scientists found that many psychics could describe places in detail when they knew the coordinates, even though they had never been there. Most scientific studies, however, have not shown that psychic ability is real.

But does psychic ability need to be scientifically proven for us to believe that it exists? Human cultures have always had psychics, for example, shamans in Latin America, fortune-tellers in Europe, and witch doctors in Africa. If psychic ability has been found in all times and places, can this mean the ability is real?

1. Does the text make you think that psychic ability is scientific? Why or why not? ______________________________

____

2. If scientific studies haven't shown that psychic ability is real, why do people still go to psychics? ______________________________

____

3. The text says, "Human cultures have always had psychics." Who are the psychics in cultures that you know about? Do you know people who have used these psychics? ______________________________

____

B. VOCABULARY FOR COMPREHENSION

Read the sentences. Below each item, write the related sentence from the box. The first one has been done for you.

He lost his ability to walk.
She needs to develop her style.
I just have a bad gut feeling about him.
~~She must be psychic!~~
Those senses almost disappear.
You need to train your ears to hear them and your mouth to say them.
Now he doesn't trust them.

1. I called Jill yesterday. When she answered the phone, she said, "Hi, Nicole." How did she know it was me?

   She must be psychic!

2. After the accident, Kurt couldn't move his legs.

   ____

3. Jackson won't go near dogs because he got bitten once.

   ____

4. When I get a bad cold, I can't smell or taste anything.

   ____

5. Alexandra is a good dancer, but she is young. She is not ready to be on stage.

   ____

6. It is difficult to learn all of the sounds in a new language.

   ____

7. I don't know why I don't like that man.

   ____

3

READING ONE: Developing Your Psychic Ability

A. INTRODUCING THE TOPIC

The title of the article is "Developing Your Psychic Ability." Write four questions about psychic ability that you think the article might answer.

1. ______________________________
2. ______________________________
3. ______________________________
4. ______________________________

Read the article and see if it answers the questions you wrote.

Developing Your Psychic Ability

1 Psychics are people who can get information about people, places, or situations through a sixth sense—a sense that exists in addition to those of seeing, hearing, smelling, tasting, and touching. They can use their psychic ability to heal people who are sick, to give advice, to give hints about the future, and to do many other things. And it's not just individuals who use psychics; sometimes companies and governments use psychics, too. One year a company called Delphi and Associates earned $120,000 on the stock market with the help of psychics. And the CIA (the U.S. Central Intelligence Agency) got help from a psychic in the 1970s. This psychic was able to make a detailed drawing of an important place in Russia.

2 "So how can I get some psychic help?" you may ask yourself. Well, you don't have to pay a lot of money to a professional psychic. You can start by using your own psychic ability. Everyone has a psychic sense, but most of us never learn to use it. You probably won't immediately be able to draw detailed pictures of faraway places you have never visited, but your psychic sense can help you in other ways. For example, maybe you will make better choices about a job, or maybe you will "know" when there is something wrong and you need to call home right away.

3 Psychic abilities are really just another sense, similar to our other five senses. The difference is that we never develop our psychic sense in the same way that we

develop our other senses. We train our eyes to see the difference between a *V* and a *U*; we train our ears to hear the difference between a /ch/ and a /sh/ sound; we can feel the difference between silk and leather; we can smell and taste if milk is sour. But our sixth sense, our psychic sense, seldom develops very much. Because most of us ignore our psychic sense for so long, it takes some time to develop it. If you have never played soccer before, you cannot expect to be a good player after three lessons. It might take years to become really good. Psychic ability works the same way.

4 To prepare yourself to work on your psychic development, you will need to do several things, including the following:

- **Make time to be alone.** It is difficult to concentrate with other people around.
- **Pay attention to nature.** Nature will give you more inspiration than man-made objects.
- **Learn to trust your "gut feelings."** As adults, we have often lost touch with our "gut feelings." To develop your psychic powers, you need to try to turn off your brain, eyes, ears, etc., and feel those gut feelings again.
- **Develop your imagination.** Developing your imagination will help you to develop your psychic ability. An important step is to turn off your TV. When we watch TV, our imagination and our psychic sense grow very lazy.[1]

5 A good teacher or book can give you some exercises to gradually develop and control your psychic ability. You may be surprised at the things you can "see" in people, places, or situations once you know how to look with your "psychic third eye."

[1] Suggestions are based on Carl Rider, *How to Improve Your Psychic Power* (Secaucus: Carol Publishing Group, 1988).

B. READING FOR MAIN IDEAS

Circle the letter of the correct word or phrase.

1. ________ people learn to use their psychic ability.

a. Many
b. Few

2. People use psychics ________ .

a. mainly to see the future
b. for many reasons

3. ________ people have psychic abilities which can be useful.

a. All
b. Some

4. Psychic abilities are basically ________ other senses.

   a. similar to
   b. different from

5. It takes a ________ to develop psychic powers.

   a. lot of time
   b. very short time

6. To develop your psychic powers, you need to ________ .

   a. make better use of all your senses to notice all the things around you
   b. concentrate and pay attention to some things we often don't pay attention to

C. READING FOR DETAILS

The article gives many examples to support the main ideas. List the examples below each statement. The first one has been done for you.

1. Give three examples of ways psychics use their ability.

   a. to heal people who are sick
   b. ________________________________
   c. ________________________________

2. Give two examples of companies and government offices that were helped by someone's psychic ability.

   a. ________________________________
   b. ________________________________

3. Give two examples of ways that psychic abilities can help us in our daily lives.

   a. ________________________________
   b. ________________________________

4. Give four examples of the things you will need to do to prepare yourself to work on your psychic development.

   a. ________________________________
   b. ________________________________
   c. ________________________________
   d. ________________________________

D. READING BETWEEN THE LINES

Decide if the sentences are true or false according to the information given in the article. Write **T** *to* **F** *next to each sentence. Then discuss your answers with a partner.*

_____ **1.** Psychics don't use their senses of seeing, hearing, touching, tasting, and smelling.

_____ **2.** Psychic ability is more difficult to train than other senses.

_____ **3.** Psychics are very rich because they know how to use their psychic ability to make money.

_____ **4.** Any person can become a professional psychic if he or she trains the psychic senses.

_____ **5.** Psychic ability may help someone choose a boyfriend or girlfriend.

_____ **6.** We can't use our psychic ability when the TV is on.

4 READING TWO: Exercises to Develop Your Psychic Ability

A. EXPANDING THE TOPIC

The following exercises are from a book about how to develop your psychic ability. Read the exercises, and then write the answers to the questions that follow. Discuss your answers with a partner. If you want, try to do the exercises!

Exercise 1

change A | to B ♈

1. Look at shapes A and B.
2. Cover up shape B and look at shape A.
3. Try to imagine shape A slowly changing into shape B.
4. Try to imagine the same thing, but make the shape change faster.

Exercise 2

1. Choose ten to fifteen photos of different people you know well (e.g., family members or good friends). Make sure that the photos are the same size. And make sure that each photo only has one person in it.
2. Put the photos in a box and mix them up.
3. Without looking, choose a photo from the box and put it into an envelope. Make sure that you don't know which photo you have chosen.
4. Take the envelope to a quiet, relaxing place. Light a candle and put the envelope next to the candle.
5. Now sit very still and let thoughts go through your mind. Don't try to guess who is in the picture. Just relax your mind. If you have one thought that seems stronger than the others, remember it, even if you think it is not important.
6. Pick up the envelope and hold it in your hands. What thoughts do you have now?
7. Stand up, blow out the candle, and open the envelope.

(continued on next page)

Is there a connection between the person in the picture and the thoughts or images that passed through your mind? Think hard. Sometimes the connection doesn't seem very important. (For example, perhaps you had an image of a small, green car and your sister in the picture borrowed a small, green car to pick you up at the airport one day. Maybe the green car isn't the most important thing in her life, but there is a connection.)

You have just "read" a photo. With practice you can begin to read other objects.

Exercises adapted with permission from Carl Rider, *How to Improve Your Psychic Power* (Secaucus: Carol Publishing Group, 1988).

1. Do you think that exercises like these could help you to develop your psychic abilities? Why or why not? ______________________________

____

____

2. If you tried the exercises, what happened? ______________________

____

B. LINKING READINGS ONE AND TWO

Complete the list in the first column. Then complete the rest of the boxes in the chart by answering each question with **Yes** *or* **No**. *Discuss the chart and the question that follows with a partner.*

The article told us that in order to develop our psychic powers, we need to:	Does exercise 1 involve/help you with this?	Does exercise 2 involve/help you with this?
1.		
2.		
3.		
4.		

Can you think of other activities you do which help you to do one or more of the things listed in the first column of the chart?

____

____

____

5 REVIEWING LANGUAGE

A. EXPLORING LANGUAGE

Complete each sentence with the letter of the phrase that fits best.

1. Troy quit smoking gradually _____ .
2. When he was a child, his imagination was really active, _____ .
3. He developed his writing ability _____ .
4. He ignored her when they met, _____ .
5. Nobody gave him any hints, _____ .
6. He had a clear image of the place _____ .
7. I couldn't trust him _____ .
8. I couldn't concentrate _____ .

a. and he was always making up great stories

b. and he acted like a stranger

c. by practicing a lot

d. because he so often told lies

e. so the party was a complete surprise to him

f. instead of all at once

g. just from hearing a description

h. when the music was on

B. WORKING WITH WORDS

Complete the following letter with the words provided.

ability	gradually	ignored	psychic
concentrate	gut feeling	imaginations	training
develop	hints		

February 4

Dear Stacy:

How are you? It's a long time since we have talked, but I have been thinking about you. I need to tell you a little about what is going on in my life right now.

You always told me that I should study art, but I (1) ______________ your advice because I didn't think that I would be very good at it. Well, a month ago, I visited a (2) ______________ who told me the same thing! I thought about how much I wanted to study art and—guess what—now I am enrolled in a couple of art classes! Actually, I started with three classes, but I didn't like one of the teachers. I had a bad (3) ______________ about him—he made me a little nervous. But the other teachers are great. I think that they will really help me to (4) ______________ my (5) ______________. The classes are quite different. In drawing class, we are (6) ______________ our eyes and hands. It's really hard work! The class is four hours long. I find it very difficult to (7) ______________ for so long. In my painting class, we use our (8) ______________ more. The teacher gives us little (9) ______________ to help us, but mostly we work on our own.

I am (10) ______________ getting better, but it will be a long time before I am really good like you!

I hope you are well.

Love,
Will

6 SKILLS FOR EXPRESSION

A. GRAMMAR: Expressing Future Predictions and Plans

1 *Read about Diane's visit to a psychic named Miriem. Each sentence includes at least one verb form to talk about the future.*

Miriem looked into her crystal ball and said to Diane, "You won't be at your job for very long. Your work is going to change completely. You will start to write—a writing project. It will start at a meeting in April. Are you traveling to a meeting in April?" she asked.

"No, I'm attending a big software developers' meeting in Dallas in March, but no, nothing in April . . ." Diane answered.

"The important meeting isn't going to be big. It'll be small," the psychic said, shaking her head a bit. "You are going to meet with two people—a man and a woman. They will help you make this change . . . ."

Write an example of each of the three different forms used to talk about the future.

____

____

____

FOCUS ON GRAMMAR

See The Future With *Will, Be Going To,* and The Present Progressive in *Focus on Grammar, Basic.*

Expressing Future Plans and Predictions

There are different ways to talk about the **future** in English.

1. Use ***will*** + **base form of verb** for predictions.	**Will** I **earn** a lot of money in this new job? (prediction –question) You **will have** money soon. (prediction) You **won't be** at your job for very long. (prediction)

Do not use *will* + base form of verb for plans made before now.

WRONG: I can't come to dinner with you tonight because I will go to a meeting.

2. Use ***be going to*** + **base form of verb** for predictions and also for plans made before now.	**Am I going to earn** a lot of money at this new job? (prediction—question) Your work **is going to change** completely. (prediction) **I'm not going to attend** any big meetings in April. (plan)
3. Use the **present progressive—*be* + *-ing* form of verb**—for plans made before now (especially plans about movement and transportation).	**Are you traveling** to a meeting in April? (plan—question) **I'm attending** a big software developers' meeting in Dallas in March. (plan) **I'm not attending** any big meetings in April. (plan)

Do not use the present progressive to make predictions.

WRONG: You are earning a lot of money in the future.

2 *Complete Alan's journal entry with the correct form of each verb. For each blank, two forms are possible. Use each of the three ways of expressing the future at least once.*

May 17

I've just seen a psychic named Esmeralda. Wow! She sure had some interesting things to tell me about my future!

"_______________ I _______________ soon?" was my first question.
1. (travel)

She thinks that I _______________ west. When people say "west,"
2. (go)

I always think about California or Oregon, but she says I _______________ farther. She thinks I _______________ in Asia in a couple of months.
3. (travel) 4. (be)

"_______________ I _______________ for a long time?" I asked.
5. (stay)

"No, a short time," she said. "But you ______________ (6. move) to another country soon—next year, maybe."

Well, that really surprised me! I can't move! My mother and father ______________ (7. move) here next month to be near me! They ______________ (8. arrive) in three weeks. I ______________ (9. take) five days off to help them find a place to live.

I was already shocked, but when she added, "Your wife and children ______________ (10. go) to this new country with you," I thought I was going to faint. I ______________ (11. not get) married any time soon! Esmeralda asked if I wanted to know any more, but I had heard enough! I wonder if all of her predictions ______________ (12. come true).

3 *Write four sentences about your plans for next year. Make sure you use appropriate forms for talking about the future.*

Example: I'm meeting my Dad for a week in Yellowstone Park in May.

1. ______________________________
2. ______________________________
3. ______________________________
4. ______________________________

Now write six questions about your future. For items 1 to 4, use the words given. For items 5 and 6, write your own questions. Make sure you use appropriate forms.

1. earn/lots of money/my life?

   ____

2. How many/children/have?

   ____

3. What/job/be?

   ____

4. own/house?

____

5. ____

6. ____

4 *Test your psychic abilities! Trade questions with a partner. Read your partner's questions. Close your eyes and concentrate on your partner carefully. Write six predictions for your partner, answering his or her questions.*

Example: I think you are going to/will have three children.

1. ____
2. ____
3. ____
4. ____
5. ____
6. ____

B. STYLE: Using Examples

1 *Look at the following two passages from the reading in Section 2A, page 179, and Reading One. Each uses examples to make a general statement clearer. In each passage, underline the examples and circle the general statement.*

Human cultures have always had psychics, for example, shamans in Latin America, fortune-tellers in Europe, and witch doctors in Africa.

. . . sometimes companies and governments use psychics, too. One year a company called Delphi and Associates earned $120,000 on the stock market with the help of psychics. And the CIA (the U.S. Central Intelligence Agency) got help from a psychic in the 1970s. This psychic was able to make a detailed drawing of an important place in Russia.

Using Examples

There are two ways to use **examples** when you write.

1. If examples are short, you can include them in the sentence with the general statement.

   Human cultures have always had psychics, for example,
   general statement

   shamans in Latin America, fortune-tellers in Europe, and
   example 1 example 2

   witch doctors in Africa.
   example 3

2. You can put the examples in separate sentences following the sentence with the general statement.

general statement	. . . sometimes companies and governments use psychics, too.
example 1	One year a company called Delphi and Associates earned $120,000 on the stock market with the help of psychics.
example 2	And the CIA got help from a psychic in the 1970s. This psychic was able to make a detailed drawing of an important place in Russia.

You can use *for example* plus a comma to introduce the first example in both cases. But it is not necessary when your example is a whole sentence.

2 *Finish the sentences with appropriate examples.*

1. There are several places I like to go to be alone, for example, ____________________, ____________________, and ____________________.

2. When I watch TV, I avoid the really stupid shows, for example, ____________________, ____________________, and ____________________.

3. My friend loves nature. She has taken several great backpacking trips to interesting places, for example, ____________________, ____________________, and ____________________.

4. Children often like to play games in which they use their imaginations, for example, ____________________, ____________________, and ____________________.

3 *In each set of sentences, write* **G** *next to the general statement and* **EX** *next to the examples.*

1. a. ____ I have had several psychic experiences recently.
   b. ____ I woke up at 2 A.M. last night, right before the telephone rang with some bad news about my grandmother.
   c. ____ And when I got to the party on Saturday, I knew that Carol was there, even before I saw her.
2. a. ____ For example, I went to a palm reader once, and she charged me $20 for each hand!
   b. ____ Another time, I phoned a psychic on a 900 number, but I didn't know that it cost $6.00 for each minute!
   c. ____ I have had some bad experiences with psychics.
3. a. ____ When I try to visualize something, all I can think about is the problems I have at work.
   b. ____ I've tried to make predictions, but they are almost always wrong.
   c. ____ I have not had any success in developing my psychic ability.

4 *Finish the paragraphs. Write at least two more sentences.*

I have heard of people who have had psychic experiences. For example, one person ____

____

____

Another person ____

____

____

There are many things you can do if you want to prepare yourself to work on your psychic development. For example, you can ________________

____

You can also ____

____

____

And you can ____

____

____

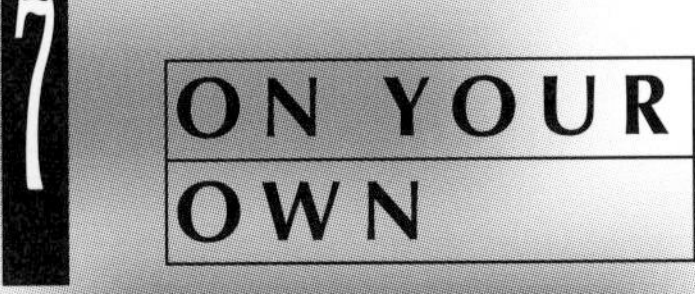

7 ON YOUR OWN

A. WRITING TOPICS

Choose one of the following topics. Write one or two paragraphs. Use some of the vocabulary, grammar, and style that you learned in this unit.

1. Write about a time when you had a psychic experience. Describe what you felt and why you thought it was a psychic experience.

2. Do you agree that people have psychic abilities? Why or why not?

3. Write about some predictions that you make for yourself for this next year. You can try to use your psychic ability. (Go to a quiet place. Light a candle. Hold a calendar for the upcoming year in your hands and turn the pages slowly. See what thoughts come to you.) Or you can just make guesses.

4. Write about an ability that you have that you have worked to develop. What have you done to develop it?

B. FIELDWORK

Work in groups. Write a survey to find out more about what people in your community think about psychics.

1. Write five *yes/no* questions, and make a questionnaire. (See the following example.)

2. Follow the procedure outlined in Unit 6, Section 7B, pages 117–118.

3. After you have finished, report back to the class about what you learned from your survey.

✶ SAMPLE SURVEY ✶

Please take a few minutes to answer the following questions.
Thank you very much!

			Comments
1. Do you believe that psychics can give you important information?	❑ YES	❑ NO	
2. Do you think that psychics can tell the future?	❑ YES	❑ NO	
3. Have you ever visited a psychic?	❑ YES	❑ NO	
4. Do you know anyone who has psychic abilities?	❑ YES	❑ NO	
5. Do you believe that you have psychic abilities?	❑ YES	❑ NO	

ANSWER KEY

UNIT 1 ◆ FINDING THE IDEAL JOB

2A. BACKGROUND

1. Most job satisfaction = Mexico
   Least job satisfaction = Singapore
2. Answers will vary.
3. Changing a job means finding a new business or place to work within the same area of interest. For example, a teacher may change her job by moving to a new school. But she is still a teacher. Changing a career means finding a new area of interest. For example, a teacher may decide to become a lawyer.

4.–5. Answers will vary.

2B. VOCABULARY FOR COMPREHENSION

2. expert
3. career
4. résumé
5. skill
6. advice
7. hire
8. want ads
9. rewards
10. update
11. manager
12. interview

3A. INTRODUCING THE TOPIC

Answers will vary.

3B. READING FOR MAIN IDEAS

1. F
2. F
3. T
4. T
5. F

3C. READING FOR DETAILS

<u>WHAT MANY PEOPLE DO TO FIND A JOB</u>

answer newspaper want ads
ask friends to help find a job
go to an employment agency

<u>WHAT BOLLES SAYS WILL HELP YOU FIND A JOB</u>

decide what kind of job is ideal
do exercises
think about your skills
think about job rewards
decide what kind of place you want to work in

3D. READING BETWEEN THE LINES

(Suggested answers. Encourage discussion.)

1. a
2. b
3. b
4. b
5. a

4A. EXPANDING THE TOPIC

2. Amanda
3. Betsy
4. Amanda
5. Betsy
6. Donna

4B. LINKING READINGS ONE AND TWO

(Suggested answers. Encourage discussion.)

1. Betsy
   Setting: I like to work with other people. I like to have my own business.
   Rewards: I like making a lot of money.
2. Amanda
   Skills: I like to help people meet. I am good at making matches. I am good at helping people.
   Setting: I like to work for myself. I like to work at home.
   Rewards: I don't need very much money. I live a simple life. I get a lot of joy from my work.
3. Donna
   Skills: I know how to skydive. I can help people learn.
   Setting: I like to work outside. I like to work with people.
   Rewards: I don't need a lot of money. I would do it without being paid.
4. Answers will vary.

5A. EXPLORING LANGUAGE

2. skill
3. secretary
4. city
5. water
6. manager
7. school
8. newspaper
9. computers
10. exercises
11. job hunter

5B. WORKING WITH WORDS

1. out of work
2. interview
3. hire
4. résumé
5. specific
6. skills

6A. GRAMMAR

1 Descriptive adjectives: new, small, great, fun, bored, interesting
Possessive adjectives: my, your, your, my

2
2. She didn't like her old job.
3. Our old manager was nice. (Also possible: Our nice manager was old.)
4. Juan found his new job in the want ads.
5. My sister is out of work.
6. Nelson Bolles has an interesting job.

3 (Suggested answers. Encourage discussion.)
2. The woman: The woman is sleepy. She has curly hair. The desk: Her desk is messy. She has a big desk.
3. The doctor: He is young. The doctor is tall. He has short hair. The patient: The patient is old. Her hair is short.

6B. STYLE

1 Sentences: 1, 3, 4
Not Sentences: 2, 5

2
2. She *is* happy with her job at the camera company.
3. *She* decided to change her job anyway.
4. Her friends told *her* to stay with the camera company.
5. *They* didn't understand her decision.
6. Why did she change her job*?*
7. Marika just wanted her dream job.
8. Marika started her own restaurant.
9. Marika *is* happier now than ever before!

3 Answers will vary.

UNIT 2 ◆
GUARDING NATURE WITH GREENBELTS

2A. BACKGROUND

1. They liked to live in cities, towns, and farms. They lived in cities because they wanted to be close to shops, schools, banks, etc.
2. They moved to the suburbs because they had cars.
3. Open space or large nature areas used to be between cities.
4. More towns and suburbs are often between cities now.

5.–6. Answers will vary.

2B. VOCABULARY FOR COMPREHENSION

2. suburbs
3. disappear
4. Suburban sprawl
5. include
6. acre
7. benefit
8. Open land

3B. READING FOR MAIN IDEAS

1. a 2. b 3. a

3C. READING FOR DETAILS

2. The size of the *Greenbelt* is 3.75 million acres. OR The size of the San Francisco Bay Area is 4.5 million acres.
3. The largest city in the San Francisco Bay Area is *San Jose.*
4. *Five hundred seventy thousand acres of the* Greenbelt is in danger.
5. The *urban and suburban area* will almost double if 570,000 acres of the Greenbelt become suburbs.
6. The Greenbelt Alliance tries to convince people *not* to build on open land. OR The Greenbelt Alliance tries to convince people to build on *land that is already urban.*
7. If you want to become a Greenbelt Alliance *member*, you must pay $35.

3D. READING BETWEEN THE LINES

(Suggested answers. Encourage discussion.)
The Greenbelt Alliance might support:
1 (They encourage building on land that is already urban.)
4 (This would make the city a better place to live.)
5 (They like to educate people about nature.)
6 (Although it includes some building, it would probably encourage more people to appreciate nature.)

The Greenbelt Alliance might not support:
1 (They don't want more building on open land.)
3 (A new highway would make it easier for people to commute from farther away.)

4A. EXPANDING THE TOPIC

1. She started it to save the forest.
2. The forest won't grow back and people will have no more wood for heating and cooking.

4B. LINKING READINGS ONE AND TWO

<u>SAN FRANCISCO'S GREENBELT ALLIANCE</u>

1. 1958
2. open land
3. people want to build more buildings

4. working with builders; working with governments; helping towns buy land; teaching people about the Greenbelt
5. space for biking, hiking, and walking; places for plants and animals; cleaner air and water; separate towns; income from farms

KENYA'S GREENBELT MOVEMENT

1. 1977
2. forest
3. people cut down trees for cooking and heating
4. planting trees
5. It gives wood for cooking and heating. It gives income to women who sell trees.

1.–3. Answers will vary.

5A. EXPLORING LANGUAGE

2. a	4. b	6. a	8. c
3. a	5. b	7. a	

5B. WORKING WITH WORDS

1. suburbs	7. includes
2. convince	8. acres
3. benefits	9. disappear
4. separate	10. urban
5. members	11. camping
6. greenbelt	12. open land

6A. GRAMMAR

1 lived, weren't, built, wanted, started, traveled, didn't need, worked, moved, began.

2

1. helped	5. convinced
2. worked	6. took
3. taught	7. didn't try
4. started	8. tried

3
2. In 1940, the towns didn't touch each other.
3. Before, the towns were separate.
4. The urban and suburban area grew a lot between 1940 and 1990.
5. In 1940, cities and suburban sprawl didn't cover a lot of the flat area.
6. In 1940, the Bay Area didn't have many people.

6B. STYLE

2
1. $3\frac{1}{3}$ - 3.333
2. 300 + 700 = 1,000
3. Where is Kenya?
4. Kenya is a country in East Africa.
5. The Kalahari, the Sahara, and the Chalbi are deserts in Africa.
6. The Sahara is in the north; the Kalahari is in the south; the Chalbi is in the east.
7. Wangari Maathai has done many things to help make Kenya a better place to live:
   - She started Kenya's Greenbelt Movement.
   - She stopped a skyscraper from being built in the middle of a park in Nairobi (Nairobi is the capital of Kenya).
   - She tries to convince politicians to do things to save Kenya's forests, animals, and people.
8. "Deforestation" means that the forest is disappearing from an area; "desertification" means that an area is becoming desert.
9. Africa's deserts are disappearing quickly.

3 (Suggested answers. Answers will vary.)
When I was a child in Morocco, I spent a lot of time in nature because my town was in an oasis. The oasis is 15.5 km long, so we could go for long walks. My favorite place to go was the river at the end of the oasis. My friends and I used to go swimming, have picnics, play soccer, and study there. Old women sometimes went there to pick herbs; shepherds brought their sheep there for water; young women sometimes went there to wash their clothes. Have you ever been to Morocco? I hope you'll be able to go one day.

UNIT 3 ◆ MAKING MONEY

2A. BACKGROUND

1. They found $18 million in fake money.
2. Counterfeiters threw out all the money.

2B. VOCABULARY FOR COMPREHENSION

1. bills: pieces of paper money
2. fake: copy of a valuable object
3. counterfeiters: people who make fake money
4. printing presses: machines that put words on paper for books, newspapers, etc.
5. scanners: machines that put a photograph onto a computer

3A. INTRODUCING THE TOPIC

Answers will vary.

3B. READING FOR MAIN IDEAS

1

b. 5	d. 7	f. 2
c. 1	e. 4	g. 6

2 c

3C. READING FOR DETAILS

1. skills, equipment
2. copier
3. special line
4. red, blue
5. ten, 50
6. yellow

3D. READING BETWEEN THE LINES

(Suggested answers. Encourage discussion.)

1. T
2. T
3. T
4. T
5. T
6. T

4A. EXPANDING THE TOPIC

1. "It" refers to counterfeit money.
2. Ben Franklin is the portrait on the $100 bill. The copy of the portrait didn't look right.
3. "Them" refers to the Secret Service agents.
4. Encourage discussion. It means getting caught doing something bad—like a child who is caught stealing cookies with his hand still in the cookie jar. There is no way for the child to say he isn't stealing.

4B. LINKING READINGS ONE AND TWO

(Suggested answers. Encourage discussion.)

	CASUAL COUNTERFEITERS	PROFESSIONAL COUNTERFEITERS
1.	✓	
2.		✓
3.		✓
4.		✓
5.		✓
6.	✓	
7.	✓	

5A. EXPLORING LANGUAGE

(Suggested answers. Encourage discussion.)

Joe's Photography Lab
portrait
scanner
bill
magnifying glass

Kwik Kopy
ink
scanner
bill

Northhampton Police Department
counterfeit
thief
magnifying glass

The *Star Daily*
ink
press
scanner

Bureau of Engraving and Printing
counterfeit
ink
press
magnifying glass
bill
portrait

5B. WORKING WITH WORDS

1. equipment
2. portrait
3. skill
4. scanner
5. fake
6. bill
7. casual

6A. GRAMMAR

❶
1. faster, easier, smarter
2. than

❷
2. worse
3. better
4. crazier
5. smarter
6. more dangerous
7. easier
8. faster

❸ (Suggested answers. Encourage discussion.)
2. The scanner is more expensive than the pen.
3. The pen is slower than the scanner.
4. The pen is more difficult to use than the scanner.
5.–11. Answers will vary

6B. STYLE

❶ **a.** 1 **b.** 2

❷
1. too
2. In contrast OR However
3. In addition OR Also
4. In contrast OR However
5. In addition OR Also
6. However

❸ 2, 1, 3

❹ (Suggested answer. Encourage discussion.)
The pen is cheaper. However, the scanner is stronger than the pen. It will last for ten years. Also, the scanner is faster than the pen. In addition, the scanner is easier to use than the pen. I think we should buy the scanner.

UNIT 4 ◆ SAVE THE ELEPHANTS

1B. SHARING INFORMATION

Extinct	Endangered	Not in Danger
mammoth	owl	horse
dinosaur	panda	crow
pterodactyl	tiger	deer
	elephant	

2A. BACKGROUND

1. All these animals are endangered because people are cutting down the trees which give the animals homes and food. Also, people are hunting the animals.
2. Friends of the Tiger and the other groups are trying to protect the animals.
3. Answers will vary.

2B. VOCABULARY FOR COMPREHENSION

2. They are endangered.
3. They are native to Africa.
4. These people are hunters.
5. They are called tusks.
6. It is made from ivory.
7. They protect the animals. These people are guards.

3A. INTRODUCING THE TOPIC

1. A friend of the Save the Elephants Fund
2. Mark Gow, Executive Director
3. A donation

3B. READING FOR MAIN IDEAS

1. The purpose of Save the Elephants Fund is to protect elephants all over the world.
2. The elephants are endangered because they don't have enough to eat and because poachers kill them. They don't have enough to eat because wood companies cut down the trees elephants eat in order to plant eucalyptus trees.
3. Save the Elephants Fund can teach companies to grow trees that are good for business and good for elephants. It can pay for guards to protect the elephants and convince people around the world not to buy ivory. Also, Save the Elephants Fund can help poachers find other ways to make money.

3C. READING FOR DETAILS

1. T	3. F	5. F
2. F	4. T	6. T

3D. READING BETWEEN THE LINES

1. No. He doesn't use his or her name.
2. Save the Elephants Fund wants money to help protect elephants.
3. They want to show readers that elephants are endangered animals.
4. If people don't buy ivory, then poachers won't kill elephants for tusks.
5. If poachers make money in a different job, they won't kill elephants to make money.

4A. EXPANDING THE TOPIC

1. He is angry because the newspaper didn't write about the loggers. It only wrote about the owl.
2. The government told the logging companies to stop cutting down trees in order to save the owl.
3. Because of decreased logging, loggers don't have as much work to do. Many loggers are out of work. They don't have much money.

4B. LINKING READINGS ONE AND TWO

	ASIAN ELEPHANTS	NORTHERN SPOTTED OWLS
1.	They are hunted. Their food is being cut down.	Their homes are being destroyed by logging.
2.	Plant other trees elephants can eat. Protect elephants with guards. Find other work for poachers. Convince people to stop buying ivory.	Stop or slow down logging in owl areas. (Possible: Call 1-800-SAVEOWL from the Website.)
3.	paper companies poachers ivory workers	logging companies and loggers

1. Save an Owl—Stop Logging: This driver wants to protect the owl.
   Save a Logger—Eat an Owl: This driver cares more about loggers than owls.
2. Answers will vary.

5A. EXPLORING VOCABULARY

2. dogs	7. brought into the place
3. animals	8. in the year 2010
4. save	9. in trouble
5. bird	10. horses
6. eucalyptus tree	11. animals

5B. WORKING WITH WORDS

1. native	5. by the year
2. endangered	6. convince
3. protect	7. donation
4. extinct	

6A. GRAMMAR

1 Questions A use the base form of the verb. Questions B use the third-person singular form of the verb.

2
2. What lives in the water near Hong Kong?
3. Why do Chinese white dolphins die?
4. What do elephants in Thailand like to eat?
5. When do guards protect the elephants?
6. Who kills many endangered animals every year?

❸ 2. Why do we need to save them?
3. Who kills them?
4. Why do they kill them?
5. Where do I send it?
6. Who do I write the check to?

6B. STYLE

❶

date — September 30

opening — Dear Julie,

body —

Hi. How are you? I'm having a great time!

I can't wait to show you the pictures and tell you all about our trip. You know how long I dreamed of going to Africa. I still can't believe it's real. And I really can't believe it's almost over. We have three more days before we fly home. We've seen every animal you can think of. Many of the animals we're seeing are endangered. I feel so lucky to be able to see them. This really is a trip of a lifetime.

I'll call you when we get back in town.

closing — All the best,

signature — Christine

❷

SAVE THE ELEPHANTS FUND
2354 MASSACHUSETTS AVENUE, NW
WASHINGTON, D.C. 01012

date — October 14

opening — Dear Friend of SAVE THE ELEPHANTS FUND,

body —

1 Thank you for your donation of $25 last year. Your money helped us to open a new elephant park in Kenya as part of our effort to help protect the 500,000 elephants left in Africa.

2 But elephants are endangered in other parts of the world, too, and we need your help again. This time we need you to help us in Thailand.

3 One hundred years ago, 100,000 wild elephants lived in Asia. Today there are only 30,000 Asian elephants. The situation in Thailand is especially serious. Thailand now has only 1,800–2,000 elephants. Experts believe that by the year 2010, elephants in Thailand will be extinct.

4 *Why are elephants in Thailand endangered?*

5 ◆ They don't have enough food to eat.
Paper companies cut down banana trees and bamboo. These plants are native to Thailand, and they provide elephants with food. The companies plant eucalyptus trees instead. The eucalyptus trees grow fast and provide the companies with wood for boxes and other paper products. The paper companies make a lot of money from the eucalyptus trees. But what about the elephants? They can't eat eucalyptus trees!

6 ◆ Hunters kill hundreds of wild elephants every year.
Hunting elephants is not legal in Thailand. But Thailand has poachers, hunters who kill animals even though it is not legal. These poachers make a lot of money from selling elephant tusks. The only way to get the tusk off the elephant is to kill the animal. The poachers sell the tusks to people who make furniture, jewelry, and art from the ivory in the tusks.

7 *What can we do?*

8 With your help and donation, this year we will:

- ◆ teach companies in Thailand about trees that are good for business and good for elephants.
- ◆ pay for guards to protect the elephants from poachers.
- ◆ convince people around the world not to buy things made of ivory.
- ◆ help poachers to find other ways to make money.

9 Last year you helped Kenya's elephants. This year Thailand's elephants need your help. Please send your donation today.

closing — Thank you.

Sincerely,

signature — Mark Gow

Mark Gow
Executive Director

❸ Answers will vary.

UNIT 5 ◆
SWIMMING ACROSS BORDERS

2A. BACKGROUND

1. d	**3.** b	**5.** e
2. f	**4.** c	**6.** a

2B. VOCABULARY FOR COMPREHENSION

1. a	**3.** c	**5.** b	**7.** a
2. a	**4.** c	**6.** b	

3A. INTRODUCING THE TOPIC

Answers will vary.

3B. READING FOR MAIN IDEAS

1. b **2.** c **3.** a

3C. READING FOR DETAILS

❶ 2, 1, 4, 5, 3

❷

2. 2.7	4. 10	6. 3
3. 38	5. 12	7. 30

3D. READING BETWEEN THE LINES

(Suggested answers. Encourage discussion.)

1. Yes. The extra layer of fat around her organs keeps her warm in cold water.
2. No. She faces sharks, large jelly fish, boats, and fatigue.
3. No. She swims mainly for this reason but she also just loves swimming.
4. Yes. By working together to help make her swim successful, two countries may gain more understanding and tolerance of each other.
5. Yes. Her swimming records are amazing, but her peace-making efforts help change the world for the better.

4B. LINKING READINGS ONE AND TWO

❶ **Lynne's Vita**

DATE	EVENT
1957	Born in New Hampshire
1962	Started swimming
1971	Swam 27 miles to Catalina Island
1974	Swam English Channel, broke women's and men's records
1975	Swam the Cook Strait
1977	Swam between Norway and Sweden and Sweden and Denmark
1978	Swam around Cape of Good Hope
1987	Swam the Bering Strait
1990	Swam between Argentina and Chile

❷ Answers will vary.

5A. EXPLORING LANGUAGE

2. e
3. a
4. c
5. d
6. f

5B. WORKING WITH WORDS

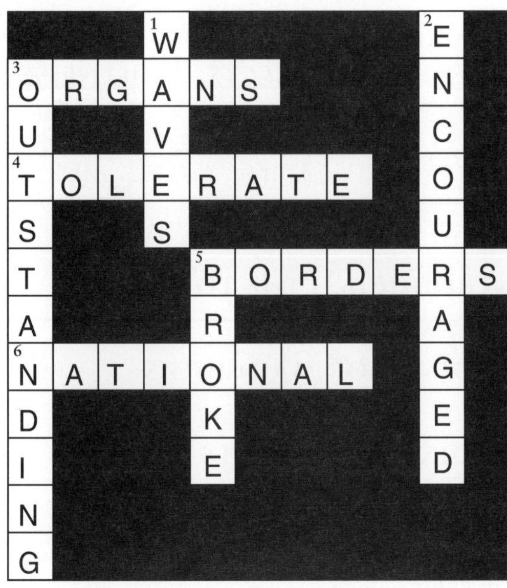

6A. GRAMMAR

1
1. The present progressive.
2. They end in *-ing*.
3. Actions that are happening now.

2
2. Robin isn't biking across America.
3. They aren't playing soccer in the park.
4. We're trying to win this game.

3
3. 'm not watching
4. 's throwing
5. 's running
6. 're trying
7. 're not running
8. 's jumping
9. 's making
10. 's happening
11. 'm not sitting

4 (Answers will vary. Suggested answers.)
The woman is winning the race. The people are clapping. She's smiling. A man is giving the man runner a bottle of water. The short man is falling down. Some people are helping him. The sun is shining. A bird is flying by. The two men runners aren't smiling.

6B. STYLE

1 Answers will vary.

2
1. First
2. Then or Next
3. Next or Then
4. Finally

3 Answers will vary.

UNIT 6 ◆
SCRUB, SCOUR, AND SMILE!

2A. BACKGROUND

1. T 2. F 3. F 4. T

2B. VOCABULARY FOR COMPREHENSION

to clean the windows (glass cleaner)
to dust the furniture (feather duster)
to make clothes whiter (bleach)
to mop the floor (mop)
to polish a silver cup (silver polish)
to scrub a pot or skillet (steel wool scouring pad)
to scrub the tub or sink (cleanser)
to wash dishes (dish soap)
to wash clothes (laundry detergent)
to wax the furniture (furniture wax)
to wipe the table (sponge)

3A. INTRODUCING THE TOPIC

(Answers will vary.)

3B. READING FOR MAIN IDEAS

2, 4

3C. READING FOR DETAILS

2. line 7
3. lines 16, 17, 18
4. lines 19, 20, 21
5. line 26
6. line 32
7. lines 33, 34, 35

3D. READING BETWEEN THE LINES

1. Advertisers: a, c, d, g
2. Poet: b, e, f, h
3. Opinion: Answers will vary.

4A. EXPANDING THE TOPIC

1. Because they have less time.
2. polishing furniture, cleaning carpets, cleaning ovens
3. laundry

4B. LINKING READINGS ONE AND TWO

Answers will vary for right-hand column answers.

polishing pots	washing the clothes
scrubbing the tub	waxing the furniture
mopping the floor	cleaning the fridge
wiping stains	cleaning the stove
washing the windows	cleaning the sink
washing the dishes	

5A. EXPLORING LANGUAGE

2. a
3. b
4. a
5. a
6. b
7. a
8. c

5B. WORKING WITH WORDS

2. Detergent, bleach
3. happen to, terribly urgent
4. glow, mop
5. mention, cleanser
6. actress, winked

6A. GRAMMAR

1 1. once a month, never, once a week, almost every day, rarely, usually, every week
2. the simple present tense

2 2. He *rarely* listens to the radio or CDs.
3. He *never* has dinner guests.
4. He is *always* in bed by 11 P.M.
5. He is *usually* at home on the weekends.
6. He vacuums the carpets *twice a week*.
7. He cleans the bathroom *three times a week*.
8. He washes the windows *every week*.
9. He cleans the oven *twice a month*.

3 Answers to questions will vary.
2. How often do you wash the dishes?
3. How often do you clean the bathroom?
4. How often do you dust the furniture?
5. How often do you stay up late?
6. How often do you invite people to your home?
7. How often do you do laundry?

6B. STYLE

2 awhile and smile
urgent and detergent

3 FLOORS: chores, doors
CLEANS: means, jeans
FUN: run, done, none
SMILE: awhile, pile, mile
MOP: pop, shop, hop, drop
SWEEP: leap, cheap, keep

UNIT 7 ◆
ORGANIC PRODUCE: IS IT WORTH THE PRICE?

2A. BACKGROUND

2. $2.49/pound	6. $1.12 each
3. $.99/pound	7. $.99 each
4. $1.59/pound	8. $2.98
5. five	9. Organic

2B. VOCABULARY FOR COMPREHENSION

1 1. d 2. a 3. e 4. b 5. c

2 Categories look like this:

CHEMICALS	*PRODUCE*	PLANTS
1. *herbicides*	1. apples	1. flowers
2. *pesticides*	2. oranges	2. vegetables
	3. broccoli	3. trees
	4. lettuce	4. *weeds*

SENSES	*INSECTS*	ILLNESSES
1. feel	1. mosquitos	1. the flu
2. smell	2. flies	2. a cold
3. hear	3. ants	3. AIDS
4. see		4. *cancer*
5. *taste*		

3A. INTRODUCING THE TOPIC

(Answers will vary.)

3B. READING FOR MAIN IDEAS

2, 3, 6

3C. READING FOR DETAILS

2. T
3. F Herbicides kill weeds.
4. F Some scientists believe that chemical buildup can cause cancer.
5. F Nonorganic fruits and vegetables are ripened with chemicals.
6. T
7. T

3D. READING BETWEEN THE LINES

(Suggested answers. Encourage discussion.)

1. organic	4. nonorganic
2. nonorganic	5. nonorganic
3. organic	6. organic

4A. EXPANDING THE TOPIC

Health Country soup is natural. Gordon's soup has artificial ingredients.

1. Health Country
2. Gordon's
3. Gordon's
4. Health Country
5. Health Country
6. potatoes, carrots, green beans, peas, onions, celery
7. broccoli, cabbage, cauliflower, spinach, green peppers, tomatoes
8. none
9. The Health Country vegetables are organic.
10. Answers will vary. Spices include: salt, pepper, parsley, nutmeg, bay leaves, sage, basil, oregano. Only Health Country has these spices, except Gordon's has salt.

11. Monosodium glutamate: chemical to improve taste. Caramel color: to give soup the "right" color.
12. Suggested answer: Health Country. It has more vegetables. All of them are organic, and it has no chemicals.

4B. LINKING READINGS ONE AND TWO

(Suggested answers. Encourage discussion.)
Price: Gordon's might be cheaper.
Taste: Gordon's might taste better because of the MSG.
Customer concerns and likes: Health Country soup has more organic vegetables.
Availability of produce: Gordon's doesn't need so many vegetables.
Time: Gordon's soup would be quicker to make.

5A. EXPLORING LANGUAGE

2. ripen
3. old-fashioned
4. produce
5. herbicides
6. pesticides
7. insects
8. natural
9. weeds
10. tastes
11. fresh

5B. WORKING WITH WORDS

2. green strawberry
3. apples
4. weeds
5. carrot
6. soup
7. hard
8. separating eggs with an electric machine

6A. GRAMMAR

1
1. lettuce, watermelon, some, a
2. spaghetti, onions, tomatoes, i, s

2
1. Singular count nouns: watermelon, cake
2. Plural count nouns: onions, tomatoes, eggs, bananas, grapes
3. Non-count nouns: spaghetti, lettuce, bread, rice, milk, fruit

3
2. rice
3. spaghetti
4. milk
5. bread
6. produce
7. lettuce
8. tomatoes
9. bananas
10. grapes
11. watermelon

4 (Suggested answers. Encourage discussion.)
4. She needs some more oil.
5. She needs some more oats.
6. She needs a green pepper.
7. She doesn't have any carrots.
8. She has a lot of walnuts.
9. She has a lot of water.

6B. STYLE

2
1. Garden Times
2. Farming News
3. Mother's World

3
2. friend
3. manager
4. manager
5. friend
6. friend
7. manager
8. manager
9. manager
10. friend

4 Answers will vary.

UNIT 8 ◆
A CHEAP WAY TO TRAVEL

2A. BACKGROUND

1. Ticket A is cheaper. Ticket A has more rules.
2. Ticket A
3. Answers will vary.

2B. VOCABULARY FOR COMPREHENSION

2. signs
3. round-trip ticket
4. counter
5. backpack
6. carry-on bag
7. luggage
8. baggage

3B. READING FOR MAIN IDEAS

1. b 2. a 3. c

3C. READING FOR DETAILS

2. He arrived at the airport *two* hours before his flight to Paris.
3. Brian had a *little* luggage.
4. Tony gave Brian a *round-trip ticket and a small package*.
5. Jean-Paul is very tall with *short*, blond, curly hair.
6. Brian paid only $110 for a *round-trip* ticket to Paris.
7. Air couriers often *can't* check luggage.
8. If a package is sent by mail, it can be *in customs* for many days.

3D. READING BETWEEN THE LINES

1. F 2. T 3. F 4. F 5. T

4A. EXPANDING THE TOPIC

1. Because she told him about very expensive tickets. He wanted information about cheaper tickets.
2. Because he wrote that he had $8000 to spend on his ticket. He made a mistake when he was typing.

4B. LINKING READINGS ONE AND TWO

Air-courier advantage: cheapest
Air-courier disadvantages: can't buy it in advance, you need to be flexible, you usually can't check luggage

Economy class advantage: cheap
Economy class disadvantage: have to buy ticket in advance, have to pay to change the ticket

Concorde advantages: very fast, good food, comfortable, limousine service
Concorde disadvantages: very expensive, only goes between New York/Paris and New York/London.

First class advantages: good food, comfortable, limousine service
First class disadvantages: very expensive

1. First class or Concorde (because of leg room)
2. Economy (She doesn't need a limousine. Most first-class/Concorde services are for adults.)
3. Concorde (She has money and is in a hurry)
4. Air courier (He probably doesn't have a lot of money.)
5. Economy or air courier (They have some flexibility, but probably not a lot of money.)

5A. EXPLORING LANGUAGE

At the travel agency	b, f, h, j
At the airline counter	d, g, i, k
On the flight	c
In customs	a, e, g

5B. WORKING WITH WORDS

1. flight
2. carry-on bag
3. disadvantage
4. luggage
5. it's worth it
6. package
7. check in for
8. check

6A. GRAMMAR

2
1. couldn't change
2. can change
3. couldn't check
4. could bring
5. can check
6. couldn't travel
7. could travel
8. can travel
9. can buy

3 (Suggested answers. Answers will vary.)

2. He can't fly economy class (because his legs are too long for regular seats).
3. She can go first class (because she has lots of money).
4. She can't go by Concorde jet (because she doesn't have much money).
5. He can't go as an air courier (because he needs to buy his ticket in advance).
6. He can't travel as an air courier (because he will have a lot of luggage).
7. She can't go first class or economy (because it takes too long).

6B. STYLE

1 Adv., Adv., Adv., Disadv.

2
2. , but
3. , but
4. , and
5. , but
6. , but
7. , and

3 Answers will vary.

UNIT 9 ◆ THE WINTER BLUES

2A. BACKGROUND

1. T 2. F 3. T 4. F

2B. VOCABULARY FOR COMPREHENSION

1. suffers
2. causes
3. lacks
4. treatments
5. symptoms
6. psychiatrist
7. common
8. affects
9. depressed

3B. READING FOR MAIN IDEAS

1. b 2. b 3. a 4. a

3C. READING FOR DETAILS

Light therapy advantages: **2.** cheapest **3.** easiest
Psychotherapy advantage: **1.** best treatment for emotional causes of SAD
Psychotherapy disadvantages: **1.** takes a long time **2.** can be expensive
Drug therapy advantage: **1.** makes most people less depressed quickly
Drug therapy disadvantage: **1.** can cause other problems

3D. READING BETWEEN THE LINES

1. T 2. F 3. F 4. T 5. F

4A. EXPANDING THE TOPIC

	JANUARY 1	JULY 1
Anchorage, Alaska	5:40	18:10
Orlando, Florida	10:22	13:96
Rørvik, Norway	3:96	21:34
Puerto Santa Cruz, Argentina	16:15	8:10
Christchurch, New Zealand	15:57	9:04
Singapore	12:01	12:54

4B. LINKING READINGS ONE AND TWO

1. Answers will vary.
2. Anchorage, Rørvik
3. Puerto Santa Cruz
4. Singapore, Orlando
5. Anchorage, Rørvik
6. chemical causes

5A. EXPLORING LANGUAGE

2. I don't think that the cat is breathing. It is probably *dead*.
3. My son has a huge appetite. He *loves* to eat.
4. Bob is trying psychotherapy to help him with his problem. He thinks that *talking to someone* will help.
5. Penny has lost weight. She looks *thinner* now.
6. The sun is really bright today. I think I need to *put on* my sunglasses.
7. Noriko and Masaki gained weight when they moved to the United States. I think they ate too many *french fries*. (Answers will vary.)
8. Mr. McDonald suffers from high blood pressure. He should eat less salt and try to relax *more*.
9. Kim had to drop out of school because he was having emotional problems. I think that he should talk to a *psychiatrist*.
10. Vanessa can't reach the teapot in her cupboard. Her husband, who is *taller* than she is, always gets it when she needs it.

5B. WORKING WITH WORDS

1. blood pressure/Emotions/affect/cause
2. temperature/common/temperature/treatment
3. depressed/appetite/lost weight/gaining weight
4. suffers/bright/symptoms/treatment

6A. GRAMMAR

2
1. shouldn't look
2. shouldn't take
3. should see
4. should sleep, shouldn't stay out
5. should exercise, shouldn't eat
6. should talk

3 (Suggested answers. Answers will vary.)
2. You should rest.
3. He shouldn't play football.
4. They should break up.
5. He should eat more.

6B. STYLE

2 So I answered, "Yes, I need to see Dr. Fong today."

"That's not possible," she said. "Dr. Fong doesn't have any free appointments for three weeks."

"Well, what should I do?" I asked. "I need to see her right away."

"What exactly is the problem?" she asked.

"I am always sleepy and I feel depressed," I said to her. "Maybe I need some antidepressant drugs," I added.

3
2. answered
3. said
4. added
5. said
6. said OR answered

4 Answers will vary.

UNIT 10 ◆ DEVELOPING YOUR PSYCHIC ABILITY

2A. BACKGROUND

1. –3. Answers will vary.

2B. VOCABULARY FOR COMPREHENSION

2. He lost his ability to walk.
3. Now he doesn't trust them.
4. Those senses almost disappear.
5. She needs to develop her style.
6. You need to train your ears to hear them and your mouth to say them.
7. I just have a bad gut feeling about him.

3B. READING FOR MAIN IDEAS

1. b 2. b 3. a 4. a 5. a 6. b

3C. READING FOR DETAILS

1. b. to give advice
   c. to give hints about the future
2. a. Delphi and Associates
   b. the CIA
3. a. Maybe you will make a better choice about a job.
   b. Maybe you will know when there is something wrong at home.
4. a. Make time to be alone
   b. Pay attention to nature.
   c. Learn to trust your gut feelings.
   d. Develop your imagination.

3D. READING BETWEEN THE LINES

1. F 2. T 3. F 4. T 5. T 6. F

4A. EXPANDING THE TOPIC

1.–2. Answers will vary.

4B. LINKING READINGS ONE AND TWO

1. Make time to be alone. (exercise 2)
2. Pay attention to nature.
3. Learn to trust your gut feelings. (exercise 2)
4. Develop your imagination. (exercise 1)

5A. EXPLORING LANGUAGE

1. f **2.** a **3.** c **4.** b **5.** e **6.** g **7.** d **8.** h

5B. WORKING WITH WORDS

1. ignored
2. psychic
3. gut feeling
4. develop
5. ability
6. training
7. concentrate
8. imaginations
9. hints
10. gradually

6A. GRAMMAR

2
1. Will (I) travel OR Am (I) going to travel
2. will go OR am going to go
3. will travel OR am going to travel
4. will be OR am going to be
5. Will (I) stay OR Am (I) going to stay
6. will move OR are going to move
7. are moving OR are going to move
8. are arriving OR are going to arrive
9. am taking OR am going to take
10. will go OR are going to go
11. am not getting OR am not going to get
12. will come true OR are going to come true

3 Answers will vary for the first four items. Composed questions will vary:

1. Will I earn lots of money in my life? OR Am I going to earn lots of money in my life?
2. How many children will I have? OR How many children am I going to have?
3. What will my job be? OR What is my job going to be?
4. Will I own a house? OR Am I going to own a house?

5.–6. Answers will vary.

6B. STYLE

2 Answers will vary.

3
1. a. G **b.** EX **c.** EX
2. a. EX **b.** EX **c.** G
3. a. EX **b.** EX **c.** G

4 Answers will vary.